RIDING THE INNOVATION WAVE

Learning to Create Value from Ideas

RIDING THE INNOVATION WAVE

Learning to Create Value from Ideas

BY

JOHN BESSANT
University of Exeter, UK

United Kingdom — North America — Japan — India — Malaysia — China

Emerald Publishing Limited
Howard House, Wagon Lane, Bingley BD16 1WA, UK

First edition 2018

Reprints and permissions service
Contact: permissions@emeraldinsight.com

British Library Cataloguing in Publication Data
A catalogue record for this book is available from the British Library

ISBN: 978-1-78714-570-2 (Print)
ISBN: 978-1-78714-569-6 (Online)
ISBN: 978-1-78714-979-3 (Epub)

ISOQAR certified
Management System,
awarded to Emerald
for adherence to
Environmental
standard
ISO 14001:2004.

Certificate Number 1985
ISO 14001

INVESTOR IN PEOPLE

CONTENTS

ACKNOWLEDGEMENTS

Writing this book has been a fascinating process and a good practical example of a valuable innovation principle — co-creation! I'd like to extend my thanks to all the people at Hella who helped to shape it, through interviews, comments and discussions, especially in and around the I-Circle. In particular, it has been a pleasure to learn from former members of Hella, including Karl-Heinz Krücken, Thomas Netterscheid, Friedrich Trowitsch, Christian Waldeyer and Eberhard Zuckmantel; and from current staff including Christian Amsel, Rolf Breidenbach, Naveen Gautam, Michael Kleinkes Bernd Münsterweg, Sabine Nierhoff, Michaela Schäfer, Christoph Söhnchen and Jason Waterman. A special thanks are due to Alexander Kerpe and colleagues at Hella Ventures Berlin for allowing me to observe a start-up starting up, and for many inspiring conversations.

Thanks are also due to Sebastian Korting and Lars Biermeyer who laboured hard in the background to support the many I-Circle meetings, and to the range of speakers and participants from across Hella who shared ideas and experiences. I'm also very grateful to colleagues from outside Hella who provided stimulating ideas and input and generously shared their experiences — Fabian Schlage (Nokia), Konstantin Gänge (Airbus), Kathrin Moeslein (FAU Errlangen-Nürnberg), Christoph Krois (Siemens), Carina Leue and Jörg Liebe (Lufthansa Systems).

I received tremendous support and encouragement from a variety of people and would especially like to thank Petra Reichel for all her kind help in organizing practical arrangements, Messrs

Burkl and Stratmann for ensuring I made the various journeys to Lippstadt successfully and to the staff at the Hella Globe for hosting so many successful I-Circle meetings. Thanks are also due to Markus Richter and Enid Nagy for their help in reviewing and commenting on earlier drafts.

I'd particularly like to mention Michael Jaeger who has been a powerful focus for innovation activity across the company and with whom I've spent some fascinating days (and evenings in the bar!) talking around the many challenges of actually making innovation happen.

Most importantly, I'd like to mention Jürgen Behrend for introducing me to the company and for sharing his deep insights into leading a large organization. At a time when we hear so much about values-based management it has been a pleasure to meet someone who lives out these principles so sincerely. I'm also grateful to him for opening my eyes and ears to the delights of German literature; he has helped fix many key insights about innovation in my mind by his use of an apposite quotation from Schiller or Goethe.

Thanks are also due to the home team at Exeter (especially Bill Russell and Allen Alexander with whom I bounced many of the ideas around), to Steve Hardman (for his helpful advice and support) and to Pete Baker and Fiona Mattison at Emerald for helping the book come to life.

And, last but not least, my huge thanks to Anna and Lara for their patience, love and support.

1

INTRODUCTION

INNOVATION — AN OLD CHALLENGE

Innovation is about survival — of course. If we don't change what we offer the world and the ways in which we create and deliver it then we may not be around for long. In a competitive environment product/service and process innovation are part of the strategic imperative.

But it's not just about being prepared to change — we have limited resources so we need to make sure the ways in which we change are the right ones and that we balance the risks and the potential rewards. And we need to think strategically about this, building for the long-term as well as dealing with short-term challenges.

We also need to be able to leverage something — we might be in the right place at the right time once but if we want to stay in the game we have to invest. Innovation is ideas — knowledge — converted into value and so we need to think about how to build and manage our knowledge base — competence.

Knowledge isn't enough — we also need to learn how to create value from it. Innovation isn't a magical event like the cartoons depicting a light-bulb magically flashing on above someone's head. It's about turning those ideas — knowledge — into value, and that involves a long and uncertain journey. We might manage to get to our destination once by sheer good fortune, but being able to make the journey repeatedly needs much more in the way of a map, provisions, experience.

Successful innovation requires careful management, organizing key behaviours into embedded routines which define the way we approach the challenges of searching for opportunities, selecting the right ones and implementing innovation against a background of uncertainty.

And finally — as if innovation wasn't already a tough enough order — we also need to be able to step back from time to time and reflect on how well we are managing it. In a changing world are our recipes, our organizational structures and processes still the right ones? Do we to keep on, cut back or develop new routines? Does our approach to managing innovation still fit the world in which we are trying to operate? Besides the capability to turn knowledge into value we need a second order capability to reflect and learn, constantly tuning our approach — what we could term *dynamic* capability.

So if we are serious about innovation then we need to be strategic in the ways we think about, organize and manage the process. Survival is not an accident.

THE DNA OF INNOVATION

In 1962 the Nobel Prize for Medicine was awarded to Frances Crick, James Watson and Maurice Wilkins for their work unravelling the structure of the DNA molecule. Together, with others in the team like Rosalind Franklin, they were able to open the door to our better understanding of genetics — how characteristics are passed on from generation to generation. A century earlier Gregor Mendel was already experimenting with these ideas in his monastery garden in Austria but the key piece of the puzzle which eluded him was the structure and operational information which the DNA model provided.

Strands of DNA make up genes and these provide the carriers for what makes an individual in terms of their make-up and behaviour — blue eyes, long legs, stronger heart, etc. Genes encode the programs for the future and being able to carry forward key characteristics enables us to survive in hostile and complex environments.

Understanding the building blocks through which genetics operates moved us to a new world where we can now engage in genetic engineering — removing troublesome genes or switching them off, splicing in new ones with additional capabilities, improving the health of existing ones.

Organizations have DNA — and we often use this metaphor. But DNA in an organization involves a set of 'programs' embedded in its structure and processes — the way we do things around here. Much organizational theory talks about 'routines' — and these are effectively the expressions of genetic coding around how we tackle the day-to-day tasks of the organization. So in the world of innovation there are routines for how we search, how we choose projects, how we manage them and so on.[1]

The big difference between an organizational model and the wider world of evolutionary genetics is that we don't have to wait for random mutations to modify the genes. Within organizations we can carry out 'genetic engineering' to revise and reshape the genes in more active ways. That's the role of leadership, trying to create organizations which are well adapted for their current and future environments.

If an organization is to survive and continue to innovate it needs to find some way of passing on its genes — continuity. And it also needs to have the capacity to review, revise and modify its genetic make-up for innovation — changing some and splicing in others, adding to the overall capability.

THE 'ONE-HUNDRED CLUB'

Needless to say not many organizations manage to do this over an extended period. Anyone might get lucky once — but whilst we hear a lot about start-ups as the exciting 'sharp end' of innovation, the reality is that most of them do not stay the distance. Growing a business from these early seeds isn't simply a matter of time — there's no guarantee of survival. It's a process fraught with challenge and based on crisis — riding the waves of change and being able to stay on top (even if its' a rough ride) rather than being drawn under.

Behind every global business there was once an entrepreneur or two — Henry Ford, William Procter and James Gamble, Bill Hewlett and Dave Packard, George Eastman — make up your own list. Making the journey from those early days to where they are today wasn't easy and involved negotiating a series of strategic challenges along the way. Leadership can take many forms, from tight hands-on control (think Steve Jobs or Jeff Bezos) through to models in which the founders continue to influence through gentle guidance, inspiring and challenging the organization as it moves forward. James Dyson was very much a hands-on founder but now plays a key role in shaping the longer-term strategic development, leaving the day-to-day running of the company to others. Richard Branson plays a similar role within Virgin as does Amancio Ortega within Inditex (Zara's parent company).

Growth inevitably requires a different approach, putting structures and processes in place where there was once fluidity and informal exchange. Striking the balance between creativity and control, between exploration and exploitation, between do better and do different — these are the day-to-day challenges of organizations moving from entrepreneurial start-up mode to long-term large-scale activity.

So it's not surprizing that relatively few organizations find themselves celebrating their 100th birthday. The challenges of innovation not only involve negotiating a turbulent world of changing technologies, markets and competition, they also involve the need for reviewing and changing the innovation model itself. Importantly this is not about simply adopting the latest management prescriptions, and following the fads and fashions of thinking about how to grow innovative businesses.

THREE KEY ELEMENTS

Smart survivors adapt and develop their own solutions, configuring from useful new external ideas and weaving these into the fabric of their own organization. They aim for continuity and flexibility and in particular they pay attention to three key strategic areas in which they build their organizational strengths (Figure 1.1):

1. *Competence* — innovation relies on new knowledge. So we need to work on building the knowledge base, not just accumulating but gardening, nurturing new shoots, trying new crops, ensuring fertile soil — and from time to time pruning and cutting back. Innovation strategy depends on managing processes of competence building (through R&D, market research, strategic alliance and network building) and on other processes

Figure 1.1. Core Elements in Long-term Innovation.

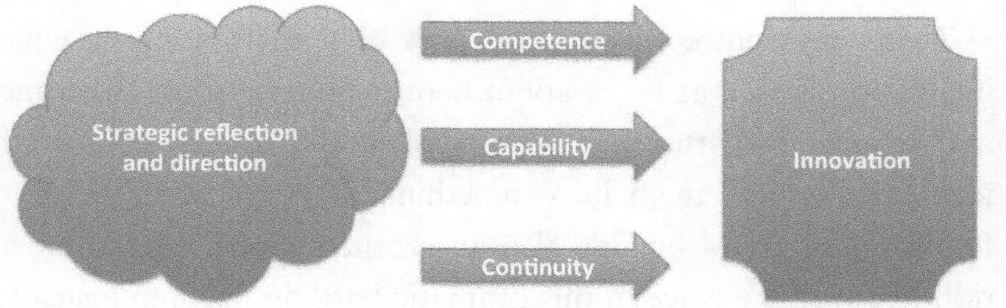

through which the knowledge base is configured and deployed to create value.

2. *Capability* — innovation isn't simply about accumulating knowledge, it is about creating value from it. Being able to do this and to repeat the trick means learning and embedding key lessons about how to make innovation happen. How to search, how to select, how to implement, how to capture value. The concept of 'routines' is helpful here — repeated and reinforced patterns of behaviour which eventually become embedded in the way we do things — our policies, procedures, processes.

3. *Continuity* — over time these approaches become the company's culture — 'the way we do things around here' representing its underlying values and beliefs. But if it is going to survive and prosper then it also needs ways of ensuring carryover of the essence of the company, understanding and transmitting its DNA to future generations.

WHO DOES THE INNOVATING?

It's easy to talk about 'the organization' as if it were a machine just running these programs — routines — for innovation. But of course it is not — organizations are made up of people and they enact the routines. Its leaders, who create and shape the context and give strategic direction, and its entrepreneurs, who enable change to happen.

These days entrepreneurs are part of a mythology in which innovation is seen as being about heroes and start-ups. Great men and women who through their passion and insight take bright ideas and wrestle them into something that creates value. It's a familiar pattern — but it's also an erroneous one. Most innovation doesn't take place in this dramatic battling fashion; instead it is a long haul, building and renewing, occasionally pushing the frontiers. Start-ups are only the beginning of what can be a long journey over constantly changing terrain.

The men and women we associate with this start-up phase may exert an influence and provide a direction and energy. But they didn't grow their businesses alone — they did so through engaging and enabling many others to help them in their entrepreneurial journey.

Entrepreneurs matter — the individuals and teams who enable innovation through their energy and passion. Innovation, as Peter Drucker pointed out, 'is what entrepreneurs do'.[2] But they mostly do it in more modest ways, working within all sorts of organizations to keep the innovation motor running. They are the agents of change, the champions who move things forward, carrying the innovation torch.

Maybe we need a new word for this character — someone who works within an organization but who is also an agent of change. Various attempts have been made — the idea of the 'intrapreneur', for example someone who is prepared to swim against the mainstream organizational tide.[3] Or 'promotor' — a label used by German researcher Eberhard Witte who suggested that we need different kinds of promotors, some with the technical knowledge to help mobilize their quest for change ('fach-promotor') and some with the power and influence to help drive it forward ('macht-promotor').[4] Others, like Roy Rothwell, use the term 'champion' — giving the sense of someone prepared to stand their ground, fight their corner and push their vision.[5] And Tom Allen's work on innovation in the NASA space programme gave us another useful label — the gatekeeper, the person at the centre of social networks and webs of influence.[6]

Whatever the label it's clear that there are many such 'everyday entrepreneurs' in our organizations and collectively they are responsible for moving the innovation agenda forward. They are different from start-up entrepreneurs in terms of the context within which they work, but also in terms of the underlying model they espouse which is less about disruption (the 'creative destruction' outlined by Joseph Schumpeter's famous theory) and more about 'creative evolution'.[7]

LEARNING FROM HISTORY

How does innovation happen? We know a lot about isolated cases, stories of breakthroughs like Post-It notes, the Model T Ford, Dyson's bag-less vacuum cleaner, the i-phone, etc. .... But how does innovation happen within organizations, what goes on below the surface events, what are the underlying routines and how do they change over time?

How do champions operate and how do they keep things moving in a context which is also about stability and resilience? How can leaders of organizations create the conditions within which champions flourish, supporting them, challenging them, stretching them — but above all not losing them because of the frustrations of working within a context that slows them down?

One source of answers is to sit on the shoulders of an organization as it goes along its innovation journey. That's the story of this book — tracking the experience of a small start-up in 19th Century Germany to its position today as a large multinational player on the innovation stage. Hella (or to give it its full title, Hella KGaA Hueck & Co) is a large German business which, despite its size (34,000 employees), wide international reach (over 125 locations in 35 countries) and large business turnover (€6.4 billion sales in 2015–2016), retains a strong sense of its origins as a family concern established over a 100 years ago in north western Germany.

Its arrival as a highly successful business today — and indeed its future — is not the result of some static feature like ownership of assets. Instead it is about the strategic development of competence — building and managing a deep knowledge base on which the company can continue to draw. It is built on capabilities to organize and manage innovation which are embedded as routines — the way we do things around here in terms of structures and processes. And it is about continuity, carrying forward the lessons of the past encoded in its DNA — the 'genetic programs' which underpin those routines.

This is a principle which the company recognizes — in the preface to its latest Annual Report it talks about the key role of innovation:

> *Innovative ideas form part of the Hella DNA and are at the same time key factors for successful differentiation in the global automotive industry. This provides us with the opportunity to take advantage of one of our core strengths and to further expand out technological leadership in response to the central megatrends of environmental and energy efficiency, safety, styling and comfort.*

Above all it is about people — and specifically multiple innovation champions — who keep things moving. They need a framework of support and an underlying value system — which in this case can be described as 'entrepreneurial responsibility'. It's a two-way thing — the expectation that employees will play a part, will take on the role of champions. And it's an expectation, a responsibility amongst senior managers to create the conditions in which they are able to do this.

It's not a simple recipe — as we'll see that the stage on which this innovation drama plays out gets ever more crowded and complex. New theatres (geographies and markets), new scenery and properties (the technology) and new audiences (new market expectations ...).

INTRODUCING HELLA

From its earliest days as a start-up in the newcomer automobile industry through to today's position as a major player, not only in automotive but also in electronics, lighting and other markets, Hella has demonstrated a continuing strand of entrepreneurship driving a steady stream of innovation.

The company consists of three business segments: Automotive (comprising Lighting and Electronics, After-market and Special Applications, with the first one accounting for the bulk of the business (**Figure 1.2**).

Lighting was where the company began and it remains one of the world's major players, with a strong history of innovation of key technologies; much of the company's current strength is based on their highly successful application of LED technology.

Electronics has moved from being a support division providing controls for lighting applications to a key pillar of the company and one where growth potential is very large. With the shift towards intelligent vehicles, driverless cars and increasing applications for comfort, security and energy efficiency have become huge opportunities for Hella to deploy its deep understanding of sensors and actuators.

Whilst a great deal of Hella's work is with the key automotive manufacturers it has also grown a strong business supplying the after-market, both in terms of spares and replacement parts and also to support workshops and garages in the increasingly technology-based world of diagnostics and repair.

Figure 1.2. Core Business Areas within Hella.

Automotive € 4804 million
Lighting € 2720 million
Electronics € 2084 million
Aftermarket € 1197 million
Special Applications € 315 million

Source: Hella Annual Report (2017).

And there is a long tradition within the company of deploying its knowledge base in related market places, providing lighting and control solutions for marine and off-road special applications.

Of course any company is more than its business units and in particular it is useful to look at Hella's corporate culture. There is a clear statement of this expressed formally as a commitment to seven basic values:

1. Entrepreneurial spirit

2. Teamwork

3. Sustainability

4. Focus on performance

5. Innovation

6. Integrity

7. Exemplary conduct on the part of all concerned

As we've seen, underpinning this is a strong emphasis on innovation and entrepreneurship — the innovation DNA.

HELLA AND INNOVATION

Hella has a strong formal commitment to innovation. Research and development expenditures were €623 million or 9.8% of sales in 2015–2016 and the number of employees working globally in R&D increased by 3% to over 6000. The message to the world is clear — Hella is a knowledge-based business. The 2016 annual report presents the company's commitment to innovation:

> *... we never stop pushing back the boundaries of what is technologically possible. We research, develop and work intensively to create innovative solutions and technologies that shape the market ....*

As the group's CEO Dr Breidenbach explains: '*Technologically leading products are key to the HELLA strategy [...] they create a competitive edge and at the same time build the foundation for our future growth*'. But the real story is not just about investment in R&D but in how to build innovation into the culture, to make it part of 'the way we do things round here'.

Over the years innovation has taken many forms. The development of new products has been a core feature but so too has change in the ways in which those products are created and delivered — process innovation. From a small local market place Hella has grown to be a major international operator and in doing so has introduced significant innovation in positioning. And it has not been afraid to rethink its core business model and to challenge and develop that as another source of innovation.

We'll explore examples of these different types of innovation in more detail in Chapter 3 but it would be good to begin by trying to trace the 'innovation red thread' which runs through the company's history.

LOOKING BACK, LOOKING FORWARD — THE NEED FOR DYNAMIC CAPABILITY

It's a disturbing statistic but surprisingly few organizations survive for long; most have a life span that is considerably less than that of a human being! Of those which do make it the one defining characteristic is change — they adapt themselves to a turbulent and constantly shifting environment. That's the innovation imperative — if we don't change what we offer the world and the ways in which we create and deliver that offering we probably won't be around for too long.[8]

For this reason we need the competence, capability and continuity outlined above. But there's more to it than that. Even those organizations that are committed to innovation, spend money on it and create supporting structures and processes to repeat the trick may still get into trouble. The challenge is one not just of innovation but of 'dynamic capability' — the ability to learn and adapt, to be prepared to review and change the approaches which the organization takes to managing the overall process.[9] It should constantly ask itself not just 'do we innovate?' but three key questions about its innovation management routines.

Of the ways in which we innovate:

- Which ones should we do more of, reinforce?

- Which ones should we do less of, or even stop?

- Which new approaches do we need to learn?

For Hella this has been the real story behind over 100 years of growth. There's a pattern, cycles of entrepreneurial exploration of new opportunities linked to systematic consolidation around them. Even though it might involve different people and take different forms, it characterizes the company's approach and is enabled by their core value of 'entrepreneurial responsibility'. This isn't an empty slogan — it is backed by real investments in giving people room and space and autonomy to be entrepreneurial.

LEARNING TO MANAGE INNOVATION

Here's a simple map of innovation space and we can use it to map the approach which Hella — or any other organization — takes to dealing with a complex environment (**Figure 1.3**).

Along the horizontal axis we move from focusing on a few well-known and understood elements in the environment to trying to deal with many unknown features. We start from a familiar world in which we know our customers, our competitors, our technologies — it's the frame within which we are comfortable and successful. But we also know that we need to explore on the right hand side, looking at new technologies, talking to new

Figure 1.3. Framing the Innovation Challenge.

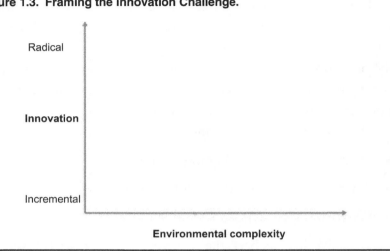

customers, watching for new competitors, learning to deal with new elements.

Along the vertical axis we are constantly trying to make innovation happen — in the products/services we offer the world, in the processes we use to do that, in the markets we serve and in our business models about how we operate to create value. This axis runs from incremental change — where we are really building on what we know, doing what we do a little better — to more radical change where we may be doing something that we (or maybe the world) have never seen before.

When we work in the zone 1 space it is essentially about incremental innovation based on exploiting what we already know. This is familiar territory in terms of technologies we understand, markets we know about, competitors whose movements we track — our job here is continuous improvement around innovations we have already established. This is, for example, Hella's core lighting business which has been continuously improving for over a century and in which it is a recognized world leader. A big part of this story is driving down the costs whilst increasing the

Figure 1.4. Exploiting Opportunities.

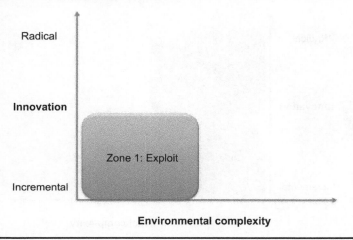

quality and differentiating the core product to meet particular user needs (Figure 1.4).

And we can push the frontiers, for example by investing further in promising technologies or working with key customers to stretch into a new generation of product. In Hella's case this might be their first moves into halogen lights, LEDs or climate control — pushing the envelope and moving the whole industry forward (Figure 1.5).

Zone 3 is very different. This is unexplored, unmapped territory, bringing new elements into the frame and combining them in new ways. It's where things interact, co-evolve and emerge. It's hard to predict innovations here — it's a soup of possibilities but it's not clear what will actually work. In innovation this is often called the 'fluid' state because it is just that — everything is moving and interacting, bubbling up with possibilities. It's classically where entrepreneurs operate, dancing amongst the opportunities, changing direction, trying and failing and then pivoting to something else which is more promising (Figure 1.6).

Figure 1.5. Pushing the Frontiers.

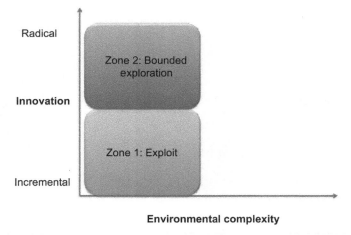

Figure 1.6. Emergence of New Possibilities.

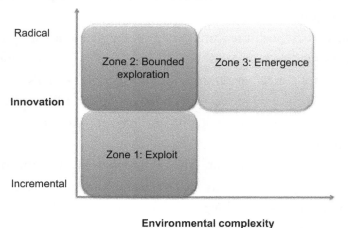

Think about the emerging automotive industry back in the 1890s, the world in which Hella was born. This was a rich soup of possibilities but no one knew how it would play out. The motor car — was it just a technological toy or a plaything for rich people? Would it really take off as a mass-market product? What would it look like — the 1890s were characterized by all sorts of ideas about cars and no clear convergence about the shape or format. What would the important technologies be and how could they come together? There was only one way to find out — try things out and see if they worked. Classic 'probe and learn' experimentation by entrepreneurs brave enough to take the risks.

Gradually the experimental ideas, the probes converge and there is a trajectory that seems to work and around which innovation moves from establishing the idea to improving on it. This is called the move to a 'dominant design' — and in the emerging auto industry it was Henry Ford's Model T which led the way. From this point the basic framework of the product became established and attention shifted to variations around that core theme and on to the big question of how to make the thing reliably and cheaply. There are still many players and many ideas involved at this stage but there is also a convergence; it's at this point that some of the key players begin to emerge and others drop out of the game (Figure 1.7).

Figure 1.7. Convergence around New Dominant Design.

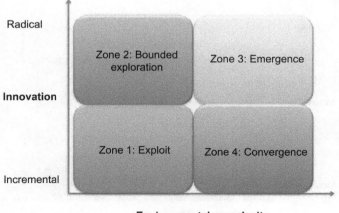

There's also plenty to do in bringing this radical new world into the mainstream, especially if we are talking about bringing something new from the right hand side into our left hand 'mainstream'. How do we bring what are, by definition, new skills, tools, technologies, knowledge sets, etc., into the established world? And how do we handle the culture clash likely to be involved? How do we bring the two worlds together?

Over time we can see a pattern, a zigzag process of innovating in different ways and in different spaces but linking things together. Today's experimental search in the right hand areas will be tomorrow's mainstream. And this means that any organization needs multiple parallel approaches to dealing with how it manages innovation. To take a simple metaphor, rather than one instrument it needs an innovation orchestra of different players who are all trying to create something together (**Figure 1.8**).

There is scope for continuous improvement approaches in the zone 1 area — and this lends itself to high involvement programmes bringing every employee into the innovation space with their ideas on how things could be improved. And there is scope

Figure 1.8. Exploring Innovation Space.

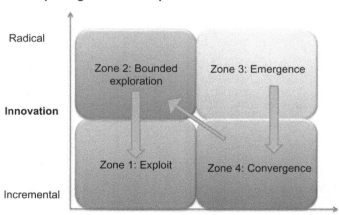

for formal R&D, pushing the frontiers in zone 2 through organized search and accompanying investment in exploring. As we move to the right so we need entrepreneurs, able to try often very different approaches, take risks and explore. And as they come up with what may be very different ideas we need business builders able to take a start-up in a very different field and develop it into something that could move across to be part of the company's future mainstream. We need scouts, able to move and make connections far away from the mainstream, and we need brokers and gatekeepers, able to connect to people 'out there' in the right hand space with interesting ideas, technologies, opportunities.

HELLA'S INNOVATION JOURNEY

That's been the pattern with Hella — from the earliest days when founder Sally Windmuller began exploring and experimenting with the new car industry, through to the post-war growth, through moving into new international markets and taking bold leaps into new technologies, like the jump into electronics in the 1980s or LEDs in the 1990s. Back in 1967 the company set up a 'Future developments' group whose remit was to explore a range of ideas which have since gone on to become standards. Importantly, this was an open search group and some of the key technologies — like heated screens — began life outside the automotive sector and were brought across from the aviation world.

This proactive approach to innovation remains a key part of the Hella strategy — for example, looking at new ways to engage employees as entrepreneurs through the 'Driving E-novation' programme, rethinking the way Advanced Engineering works to increase its agility and ability to explore new and different ideas fast, and most recently with the development of a 'disruptive innovation' capability in Berlin and Silicon Valley.

And it's been a pattern with some consistent elements, what might be called Hella's 'innovation DNA'. These strands include:

- Learning from and with growing markets has always been a key feature, from the earliest days through to building close co-operations with key automobile makers, through to today's exploration of very different market locations like China and India, and working to learn new approaches from those opportunities;

- Encouraging and supporting entrepreneurial behaviour — creating the conditions within which 'entrepreneurial responsibility' can form part of the culture;

- Sustaining a commitment to developing and growing the necessary skills to support an increasingly wide knowledge base — and doing so through investments in people and in educational systems to provide this;

- Working with external networks, linking to people outside the organization to ensure the flow of knowledge — for example, in moving into the new field of electronics back in the 1980s;

- Partnering with key technology developers, both in research centres and collaborating with competitors to help push the overall innovation frontier in key areas like advanced lighting;

- Learning about new technologies and then managing the difficult task of integrating these knowledge sets within the company — 'rewiring Hella's brain!'. The example of moving into electronics, which effectively shifted the knowledge base from mechanical engineering and lighting physics to include a completely new field (carried with it by a wave of new people), highlights the challenge here.

All of these are learned and embedded parts of the Hella approach — and in moving into the new landscape identified above will be central to the future of innovation within the business.

We'll look at these in a little more detail in the rest of the book but in the next chapter let's take a closer look at Hella's innovation history.

FURTHER RESOURCES

You can find a number of useful resources — case studies, video and audio, and tools to explore some of the themes discussed in this chapter at www.innovation-portal.info

In particular:

- Case histories of companies innovating over an extended time period — Marshalls, Dyson, Zara, 3M, Philips and Corning

- Case studies of changing patterns of innovation in various sectors over time — the imaging industry, music industry, lighting industry

- Video introduction to the idea of innovation management and a process model

REFLECTION QUESTIONS

1. Identify an organization that is a member of the '100 Club' — i.e. it has been around for over 100 years. Try and map their innovation history, key milestones, etc.

2. Use the map in Chapter 1 to look more closely at how they explore innovation space

3. Discontinuous innovation happens. And whether it is triggered by technological, market or political change the result is the same — a challenge to established players and an opportunity for entrepreneurs. Find an example of a

discontinuous shift — for example a major change in technology, markets or regulatory environment. Look at the players within that sector and explore what they did (or did not do) to ride with the waves of change. What else could they have done? Who were the newcomers trying to enter the space and how did they play their game? (You can find a framework to help with this on the Innovation Portal 'Patterns of discontinuous innovation').

NOTES

1. You can find a more detailed discussion of the idea of organizational routines for managing innovation in Joe Tidd and John Bessant (2014).

2. Drucker (1985).

3. Pinchot (1999).

4. Witte (1973).

5. Rothwell (1992).

6. Allen (1977).

7. Schumpeter (2006).

8. de Geus (1996).

9. For a more detailed discussion of this topic see Zollo and Winter (2002) and Teece and Pisano (1994).

2

HELLA'S INNOVATION HISTORY

BEING INNOVATIVE

Since 1899 HELLA has been continuously making its mark on the market with outstanding ideas. This innovative power is both the origin and the future of the company. Those who want to be global leaders must be — and stay — curious, persistent and flexible. Networking at all levels is the primary reason behind this wealth of ideas. Our employees from around the world contribute new, fresh ideas for safer products and more efficient processes day by day.

From the 2013–2014 Hella annual report

IN THE BEGINNING ...

Westphalia is good farming land spread out like a green blanket across the north-west of Germany, rolling plains and gentle forests marking the boundaries at the edges of rich fertile fields with contented cattle grazing in the afternoon sun. The year is 1877, a good time and place to be in the animal feeds business, which is where we find Sally Windmuller taking over the family's operation. They've been around a long time, can trace their roots right back to the 13th Century and are now well established in the fabric of Westphalian farming society. Plenty to do, closer personal links and reliable service are the hallmarks of Sally's work with local farmers — but for a young entrepreneur like Sally there's a sense that there is more he could do.

There are plenty of opportunities beyond animal feeds — for example, a whole population of farming clients own some form of carriage which they use to get around in. And each of these carriages is going to need various accessories — some for essential use, some for decoration. He gradually builds a business alongside the animal feeds which specializes in making and selling whips, harnesses, door handles, lamps and horns — all the fixtures and fittings without which no horse-drawn vehicle is complete.

And it works. His vision turns into a successful business, combining a variety of skills in leatherwork, metalwork and engineering and he grows the company from the original four employees selling feeds to around 120 people.[1] It wasn't an overnight success; he expanded it slowly but steadily. But by 1888 he was selling to a growing number of customers outside the region, increasingly focusing on the accessories and expanding fast enough to need a factory in which to make the volumes required. In 1895 he was able to buy up some machinery from a company called Cöppius-Schulte-Röttger which made lamps but had gone bankrupt; using this as the core he set up a factory in Lippstadt and employed 30 people making lamps for horse carriages and bicycles.

Meanwhile in another part of the country other entrepreneurs were at work pursuing their versions of dreams and opportunities. In particular two men — whom had never met but had worked along similar parallel lines for many years — were busy with their new ventures in the southwest. In 1886 Carl Benz demonstrated the world's first automobile in Mannheim while a little further up the road Gottlieb Daimler did the same in Stuttgart. Both men had been fascinated by early discoveries around the internal combustion engine and together with friends and work colleagues they explored how to create a vehicle.

Daimler joined with his friend Wilhelm Maybach fitting a kerosene powered engine to a two-wheeler car and took it for a successful test run in November 1885. Meanwhile Benz had earned enough from his 1879 stationary single stroke engine to fund his dream of creating a lightweight car powered by a gasoline engine, in which the chassis and engine formed a single unit. As a stepping stone towards a four-wheeled vehicle he developed the 'Velocipede', which he demonstrated in July 1886 after having first applied for a patent for his 'vehicle powered by a gas engine'. The patent — number 37435 — may be regarded as the birth certificate of the automobile.

The idea soon moved from demonstration to practical application; Daimler began exploring where else he could use the principle, looking at rail, marine and even aviation markets. And Benz's wife Bertha took their two teenage sons on what was probably the world's first long-distance journey, driving an improved version of her husband's car on a meandering 180-kilometre road trip in 1888. In the process she demonstrated the potential of the motor car not just as an engineering curiosity but as a practical means of transportation. It wasn't cheap but for a few wealthy early adopters it looked interesting and so both Daimler and Benz began to grow their businesses.[2]

AN OPPORTUNITY AND AN ENTREPRENEUR...

Up in Westphalia Sally Windmuller heard about this and his entrepreneur's brain clicked into gear. 'Horseless carriages' still sound like carriages — and so there might be space for him to join the party. While much of the attention by the manufacturers is on the engine and the power transmission he reasons that someone has to pay attention to the rest — the chassis and the body. That's going to need lights, horns and many of the other things he's already supplying to the mainstream carriage trade.

It's a new kind of challenge — and a high-risk opportunity. If this new idea catches on there will not only be the old business of horse-drawn carriage fixtures and fittings but also a new market for the emerging car industry. He persuades some backers and on the back of his growing success in the carriage trade he is able to set up a company in 1899 — Westfälische Metall-Industrie Aktien-Gesellschaft (WMI) — to make horns and lights for both carriages and the new horseless carriage industry.

The first cars that cruised Germany's unpaved roads in the early 1900s had lamps similar to horse coaches: paraffin, candle or gas lamps. However, lighting was not standard equipment in the already extremely expensive vehicles and was therefore considered a luxury. To drum up business, Windmuller, who was the first to own an automobile in his hometown, used his vehicle as a sales tool. He equipped his car with the lighting fixtures his company made and drove around town. He also visited trade shows in Germany and abroad, showing off WMI's products.

Characteristic of this early stage was a commitment to skills and technology; a good example was his recruiting of 40 musical instrument makers from Saxony to work in the expanding horn factory. Persuading skilled craftsmen to migrate from one side of the country to the other required considerable faith on both sides!

The company's newly established advertising department and travelling salesmen marketed WMI's products throughout Germany and Europe. By 1905, WMI was a thriving mid-sized business with almost 200 employees that exported its products to many Western European countries as well as to Hungary and Russia.

Ever the entrepreneur Sally Windmuller saw another opportunity with the emergence of the first electric light for cars. Up until then lamps were acetylene, paraffin, oil, even candles; the year 1906 saw the first light bulb suitable for use in automobiles invented by German light bulb manufacturer Osram. Two years later, WMI began to make battery-powered electric lamps for cars, including sidelights, rear lights with a red glass cover and license plate lights.

The early days of horns and simple lights drew on a simple knowledge base, one grounded in making and repairing horse-drawn buggy equipment. But soon came the need to specialize and learn to understand and control. Sally Windmuller had seen the need to invest in what we would now call R&D; for example, early on he saw a key development was going to be the new acetylene lamp — a big move forward compared to the old oil or even candle powered lights. Recognizing the importance of technology led to the award of their first patent, in 1901; although this was for a very different kind of machine to their core business it gave them valuable experience in the process of assembling and protecting intellectual property.

A more direct success from applying technology came in 1908 when the 'Hella system' was used for the first time. Based on a product developed in 1906 this involved using a foil reflector in the lamp and a focusing lens in front of the acetylene burner; it effectively doubled the range from 150 to 300 metres and heralded the era of the headlamp as opposed to a simple lamp. This design was also easier to make with higher precision and manufacturing costs were reduced.

It was also at this time that the 'Hella' brand was formally registered and the strong association with lighting emphasized. There are several ideas about where the name came from; in German the word 'hell' means light so there is a plausible link. But Sally's wife Helen was also nicknamed 'Hella' giving us another strong contender for the inspiration behind the brand. Whatever the source of the name it stuck; although the company name remained WMI until the 1980s it traded under the brand name of Hella and increasingly became associated with that.

Learning about making — process innovation — as well as about product technology was also an important early piece of the puzzle. A local firm went bankrupt and Sally Windmuller bought the firm's machinery, using it to set up a factory in Lippstadt in 1895. This provided the opportunity to learn valuable first hand lessons about factory organization and volume production.

To keep up with the growing demand, another brand-new factory was built in 1911 and WMI took on the production of additional accessories for carriages and cars, including whip holders, locks, ashtrays and a variety of handles. By 1912, subsidiaries had been established in London, Paris, Vienna, Barcelona, Milan and New York.

CRISIS AND SURVIVAL — JUST

But then came the first of many crises in Hella's history — the First World War. Alongside most of German industry the company was required to switch production to manufacture war goods, including handguns, grenades and other weapons components. This kept the business going and people employed but stifled the export trade and also forced their innovation hand in new directions. Development of product technology stopped but was replaced by a lot of fast learning about production — how to make things in high volumes to reliable quality, and quickly!

By the end of the war the company's fortunes were looking less than rosy; annual turnover in 1918—1919 stood at less than half of the pre-war levels and the prospects for growth in a war-damaged economy were not good. For Sally Windmuller this was a tough time — he'd managed to lead the company through the difficult war years but now faced the bigger challenge of keeping things going. Part of the problem was extreme shortages of key raw materials and so, in true entrepreneurial fashion, he looked far and wide to find these. In the process he ventured a little too close to the wind, approving the purchase of scrap metal, tools and other resources from German army stocks. This was illegal at the time and he was sued in 1921 with the charge of 'causing damage to the State'. He escaped jail but had to pay a heavy fine and was put on probation.

The personal damage was significant; from founding and running the company he had to step down, losing most of his assets in the process (this included the magnificent house on the edge of the factory in Lippstadt which still stands there today, now serving as the Hella Forum, a meeting place for workshops and special events). He stayed linked to the company but moved to Berlin where he ran the sales agency for Eastern Europe; he died in 1930.

For the company this was also a traumatic time. Quite apart from the day-to-day challenge of keeping the business going there was now a major economic crisis in the country. Inflation rocketed and the government issued increasing amounts of currency to manage the debt burden resulting from the war; by the time of a major currency reform in 1923, WMI, along with most of German industry, was in a very weak position — no exports, a collapsing internal market and a climate of high uncertainty.

As if that weren't enough there was also a battle for ownership and control. The original WMI investors were a mixed group and their shares had been bought in many cases by a group of bankers seeking to gain a majority shareholding. But there was also a new player in the game — the Hueck family from the nearby town of Lüdenscheid.

Founded in 1814 in the hills of Sauerland the brass and other metals business of Edward Hueck and Sons had grown from its original role making buttons to cover a wide range of industrial goods. They had pioneered steam power, built one of the first brass rolling mills in 1879 and installed Germany's first extrusion press in 1908. They continued to build their capability as a specialist supplier to — amongst others — the WMI business. One of the sons of the original founder, Oskar Eduard Hueck began buying shares in WMI after the end of the war and when the bankers tried to raise additional share capital he recruited the services of his eminent lawyer brother, Alfred. They managed to see off the challenge and after a long legal battle acquired the majority shareholding of 60%. Oskar Edward became chairman in 1923 and three years later brought in a relative (his wife's cousin), Dr Wilhelm Röpke to help him as Commercial Director.

So, WMI at least had firm hands on the tiller even if the ship was now heading for some very stormy waters. Linking with the Hueck business brought with it some valuable resources in terms of technology and production experience; for example, Oskar Edward had spent time in the United States and had learned a great deal about mass production methods which had been pioneered in the United States but were only beginning to be used in Germany. Early automation and the first use of conveyors in the factory were a feature of WMI's production in the 1920s.

RIDING ROUGH WATERS

But on the product and market front the 1920s and 1930s proved very difficult; the company moved between its 'core' business of automotive fittings and a much wider world of products. These years were essentially a fight for survival with a serious economic slump in 1925, which led to the closure of the factory for two months during 1926. The 1929 Wall St crash sent another shock wave around the world and depressed markets still further; in Hella's case their turnover in 1933 was only a third of the 1929 level and the number of employees contracted from over 800 to 250 during that period.

At a time when stock markets were crashing around the world and where depression was rolling in, the opportunities in cars were limited and Hella was forced to switch production to make anything for which there was at least some demand. They learned how to make household goods such as kettles, saucepans, cans and spoons as well as working with markets at the fringe of their auto business — products for bicycles, motorcycles and motor boats. By the early 1930s over a third of Hella's turnover came from these markets, and whilst there were some opportunities to learn about different markets, technologies and materials the impact on building core competence around automotive-related knowledge was limited.

The turning point came during the 1930s with increasing state intervention in industry. Against this backdrop the National Socialist government was forced to intervene in the economy and during the 1930s there was an increasing level of state control and direction. Tax on automobiles was abolished in 1933 and the market grew from around 120,000 vehicles to nearly four times that volume by 1938, with Hella benefitting from supplying various fittings for these. And on 28 May 1937 the '*Kraft durch Freude*' (KDF) car was launched, its name meaning 'strength through joy'; this was the forerunner of the Volkswagen 'Beetle' and had been designed to be a 'people's car' (*Volkswagen*) with an affordable price for everyone.

Hella was engaged to supply lights, indicators, horns and other components for this project — laying the foundations for what became a major relationship during the later years of growth of the company. Their expansion also included a major contract with Ford on an exclusive supply basis in 1936, and by 1939 Ford was WMI's most important customer. Business finally was improving; the company was employing over 1700 workers, up from the 250 in 1933. And, importantly, the 1930s saw a systematic investment in recruiting and training young people, laying the foundations for what is still a key commitment to the local region and ensuring a steady supply of intermediate skills to support manufacturing.

ANOTHER WAR, BACK DOWN AGAIN

But once again this steady growth was stopped in its tracks by the outbreak of war. Export markets — including the key deal with Ford — disappeared and instead 60% of turnover shifted to military applications, although this time there was a stronger emphasis on core components like headlamps rather than diverting production to armaments. Shortages of skilled labour were another problem as most of the men had been recruited into the armed forces.

By the end of the war there was again near collapse in the economy and, although Hella was permitted to continue trading, the overall German market was tiny — less than 7,000 vehicles and growing slowly. The workforce had almost disappeared; in 1945 only 45 people were on the books. In order to keep production going Hella switched once again to making anything and everything — coffee pots, crankshafts, bicycle lamps, alarm clocks, headlamps for the British Rhine army, a vegetable drying installation, a sugar beet processing plant and crop spraying equipment!

RIDING THE WAVES OF THE 'WIRTSCHAFTSWUNDER'

1948 saw the beginning of the 'Wirtschaftswunder' — the economic miracle — through which German industry began to re-establish itself. Hella's fortunes rose with the gathering tide, helped by some luck. Although some of their more sophisticated measuring equipment was confiscated the bulk of the plant and machinery remained intact and ready or use. Their pre-war links with Ford were reinstated so that they had early access to a big export market and exposure to differing customer demands. And they were able to position themselves as a technology leader — for example, by delivering the first blinking turn indicators for the Taunus and Goliath models in 1951.

The figures for vehicle production over the following decade underline this with Hella supplying a wide range of components (Table 2.1).

The relationship with Volkswagen (VW) was particularly important; in 1950 they accounted for half of Hella's sales and this rose to 60% by 1955.

The growth can also be seen in employee numbers (Table 2.2).

Table 2.1. Hella Production Figures (Number of Vehicles Supplied).

1949	163,000
1954	680,000
1959	1.7 million

Table 2.2. Employee Numbers at Hella.

1945	45
1948	1,500
1959	5,500
1961	7,000

And in exports; between 1950 and 1955, these roughly doubled. Besides going to the United States, Hella products also found their way to Austria and Switzerland, Benelux and Scandinavia. In 1957, a Brazilian manufacturer acquired a license for a number of Hella products.

But Hella's growth during this period was not simply about being part of a rapidly expanding market; they were also reaping the rewards of their continuing commitment to innovation. For example, in the product technology field they led with many key innovations including flashing indicators and lights, different headlamp shapes and geometries enabling cheaper lenses, asymmetric dipper beams and new reflector technologies.

All of this required investments in learning and competence building — in optics, mechanical engineering and especially in the emerging field of control with some of the new possibilities opened up by electronics. This was a critical turning point for Hella; although some simple electromechanical devices were in use and the company understood the basic physics behind electronics it was not until the invention of the transistor in 1947 that significant new possibilities began to appear. With the development of integrated circuits and simple programmable devices in the 1960s came the possibility for applying solid-state electronics (SSE) in a range of components. Hella was an early entrant into the marketplace with an electronic indicator flasher launched in 1965.

MAINTAINING CONTINUITY — THE FAMILY CONNECTION

Steering the ship through this ocean of new possibilities was the son of Oskar Eduard Hueck, Arnold. A physicist by training he joined the company in 1950; soon after the Hueck family negotiated to buy all the remaining shares in WMI, setting up in the process a limited company. To preserve their autonomy in decision-making the company changed its form again in 1959 to be a limited liability partnership with Arnold Hueck as executive general partner. He was joined in 1957 by Wilhelm Röpke's son, Reinhard who became another executive general partner in 1966.

These two led a small management team overseeing the growth during the years of the Wirtschaftswunder. They expanded production facilities continuously during the 1950s, adding another Lippstadt site in 1958 and moving into several other cities including Todtnau, Recklinghausen, Hamm-Bockum-Hövel and Bremen. Similar expansion in the product range included supplying windshield wiper and washer control systems, and rotating beacons for police cars and special vehicles. WMI's sales tripled during that period, passing DM 100 million in 1959 for the first time.

INTERNATIONALIZATION

As German industry gained confidence it began to move overseas and Hella was part of the early wave of suppliers internationalizing alongside their key customers like VW. But Hella had seen the potential in the global market well before that and on its own initiative had begun to move production and sales operations overseas. In 1961 WMI opened its first production facility outside Germany in Mentone, Australia and followed this with a series of moves into South America, Asia and Western Europe. The trend continued for three decades, culminating in a major eastward expansion as the Soviet Union collapsed and new facilities were established in the Czech Republic, Slovakia and Slovenia to serve these opening markets.

By the mid-1990s, Hella had become a global supplier to some of the world's biggest automakers with roughly $3 billion in sales and a workforce of 17,000. A worldwide network of production plants — often right next to the customer's assembly lines — made 'just in time' delivery possible. In 2012 Hella started a co-operation with the Chinese automobile manufacturer BAIC to develop and produce light systems, particularly designed for the Chinese market. And today HELLA operates from more than 125 locations in over 35 countries.

CRISIS STRIKES AGAIN

During the 1980s the company continued to grow and consolidate, expanding on the electronics side in particular. Another family member joined in 1987, Jürgen Behrend who was married to Arnold Hueck's daughter. Dr Behrend, a lawyer by training, had worked in the Hueck business in Ludenscheid since 1982 and was familiar at a distance with the Hella operation (in fact, he was not a newcomer to the Lippstadt site itself, having worked in holiday jobs around the workshops and driving cars for the company). He worked alongside Reinhard Röpke, overseeing some of the newer developments and providing further strength to the senior management team.

Although there was a strong hands-on approach from this strategic group (including continuing involvement of the ageing Wilhelm Röpke) this posed some challenges for Hella since decision-making was effectively concentrated at a high level, leaving the rest of the organization to focus essentially on operations and tactical decisions. The risks of this concentration were cruelly exposed in 1992 when Reinhard and his family were on a holiday in New Zealand. The light plane in which they were travelling crashed and there were no survivors; as a company Hella was effectively beheaded.

Jürgen Behrend stepped into the overall leadership role and became Liable Partner in 1993 with the support of the rest of the family. But his task was now to revitalize a company in shock at a time when major new strategic decisions were needed.

During the next years the urgent task was to steady the ship but it became clear that some major strategic surgery was also needed. In particular, the old model of leadership had placed relatively little emphasis on disciplines of strategic planning and control, and there was an urgent need to bring these disciplines into play. To bring an external perspective the management consultants McKinsey came in with a team to help review and strengthen the company's operations.

One area of particular concern was around product development. This side of the business, especially in electronics, had grown rapidly to create a very effective 'ideas engine' but one which was not well geared for delivering innovation — creating value from those ideas. A detailed analysis of the problem was commissioned and this suggested that of the roughly 4,000 products in the range at that time the vast majority took up time and effort but made little contribution.

- 95 products responsible for around 80% of turnover and 34% of R&D costs

- 305 responsible for 15% turnover and 35% R&D

- 3,100 responsible for 5% of turnover and 31% of R&D

Not only was rationalization urgently needed but also a process to develop a portfolio approach and selection criteria to allocate resources and progress projects. Around this time the concept of product managers was also introduced (there is a more detailed description of this reorganization in Chapter 3).

The big change took place in 1993, driven by Behrend, and was essentially aimed at bringing about much closer functional integration. Prior to this there were small 'empires', each working independently and only loosely connected — for example, there were no less than nine Deputy Managing Directors responsible for various areas. In particular design, planning and manufacturing were highly separated. Before 'Die Änderung' (the change) took place these had operated as very different worlds. As one interviewee explained, "*It used to be that manufacturing did what they were told, never got or gave feedback. Equally no designer knew the price of his changes — there was no cost consciousness. Neither component cost nor final selling price .... And R&D never went near Production — that was forbidden*".

Inevitably, this meant inefficient use of resources and real risks of duplication of effort. The 'change' brought the different worlds closer together — for example, measurement test equipment, which was developed and implemented in parallel with the production people.

ENTREPRENEURIAL RESPONSIBILITY

It was not just the arrival of consultants with new approaches and techniques that enables the company to adapt, much had to do with Jürgen Behrend's different beliefs about management, originally learned and tested during his time with the Hueck company in Lüdenscheid. His belief in 'entrepreneurial responsibility' — the idea that employees have much to contribute and want to do so, are motivated by this rather than simple instrumental rewards — was particularly relevant. Enabling employees to make their contribution required a similar responsibility on the part of management to create the conditions under which they could do so. This philosophy was, to some extent, at odds with the somewhat autocratic style with which the company had grown up, but in walking around and getting to know the Lippstadt plant he became convinced of the value of trying to change the culture towards this more participative approach.

Things had already started to change within the company — one important element was the shift in technology around electronics which brought about a 'changing of the guard' in terms of key players in the innovation game. In order to ride the growing wave of electronics applications there was a need to recruit new young people with no direct experience of the old WMI culture. At the same time there was a large cohort who had grown up in a more mechanical era and felt uncomfortable with the new one. In 1992 an integrated electronics team was established, bringing hardware and software engineers together and enabling further linkages across the growing knowledge base.

The emerging picture by 1996 was a shift in the underlying innovation model, away from the entrepreneurial idea-driven approach and towards one which was more customer-centric and which emphasized planning and review. Innovation became a matrix-based activity, linking different players more tightly together. There was a clear product and market strategy giving shape to future innovation activity and setting out a clear commitment by the company to continuing to invest in electronics as a growth engine. Importantly, there was also a small group (building on the original future developments organization which dated back to the 1960s) which took responsibility for exploring products and processes on the fringes of this core strategy; effectively Hella now had a large focussed development resource and a smaller future-oriented group.

A critical element in all of this was mobilizing the knowledge base of the company more effectively. Hella had built deep competence in lighting and electronics but was not necessarily getting the full benefit of this knowledge. Reorganization helped with this integration and the new Product Managers played a key role in building links and networks to specialists inside the factory.

Another aspect of the reorganization around this time was a move away from the strong centralization around the Lippstadt headquarters. Although the company had extended its international footprint it was still very much run from a German centre; the 1990s saw moves to establish strong centres in China, the United States and Mexico and to move to a flatter more global model.

HELLA IN THE 21ST CENTURY — OLD CRISES, NEW STORMS

So at the end of the company's 100th anniversary year — 1999 — Sally Windmuller's vision had paid off. A business had grown alongside the burgeoning automobile industry and he was right in his gamble that there would be a need for horns, lights and other accessories. But the business had also transformed, growing three valuable additional legs on which to stand. An after-market operation that could help balance the leads and lags and uncertainties in the core OEM world. A growing independent presence as a sophisticated supplier of technologies around electronics. And a focussed special applications business working in adjacent markets and able to leverage Hella's core knowledge base. Importantly the company was also no longer reliant on in-house capacity alone; a network of partners and joint ventures enabled them to cover a complex technological frontier.

But they were not out of the woods yet. Global drivers, especially the increasing emphasis on reducing costs by Hella's powerful customers, kept up pressure to rationalize and focus the supply base. Hella needed to step up to the plate of being a reliable top tier supplier — or get out of the game.

The first decade of the new millennium was characterized by a series of shocks — for example the company experienced a crisis in 2005–2006 due to problems in their lighting division — and a series of interventions aimed at stabilizing the ship. In particular another strong drive towards cost-cutting and increased efficiency helped them to recover in 2006–2007, only to then be hit by the after-shocks of the global financial crisis triggered by the collapse of Lehmann Brothers in 2008. This had a significant impact on world industry — for example, all the major US car-makers needed massive state aid to continue trading — but Hella's efforts at strengthening their core productivity paid off and they remained profitable in spite of these external shocks.

For Jürgen Behrend the responsibility of trying to steer the company alone was proving difficult. One member of the McKinsey team who had been helping in various ways during the late 1990s was Dr Rolf Breidenbach, with whom Jürgen had developed a good working relationship. The two kept in close touch and when Jürgen put it to the family that they needed to bring in a strategic senior manager to help him, his proposal of Breidenbach was positively received. Behrend approached Breidenbach and he joined on a full-time basis as joint Chief Executive in 2003.

This provided a welcome injection of additional strategic capability, complementing Jürgen Behrend's vision and challenges for the future with some strong operating expertize. The two began another era for the company, playing an effective double act, which balanced entrepreneurial exploration with careful concern for operations and systematic exploitation of the core knowledge base. A wave of initiatives were kicked off, exploring and stretching Hella's capability around open innovation, diversification and developing capability for dealing with disruptive innovation. But in each case the strategic push to explore was balanced by a measured assessment of the relevance of these new approaches and their configuration to make sure they fitted the Hella world.

By 2014 the company had returned to strong profitability and a key new step was taken, floating around 30% of the shares on the Frankfurt Stock Exchange. From its origins as a family business Hella moved into the wider world of the capital markets, recognizing the need for additional resources to support future growth but also acknowledging a shift away from hands-on strategic management by members of the family. In 2016 Jürgen Behrend announced his intention to step down and from October 2017 sole direction of the company would be in the hands of Rolf Breidenbach, reporting to a mixture of family and external shareholders.

CONTINUITY IN INNOVATION

Throughout its history innovation has been at the heart of Hella's approach and there has been a steady evolution of its capability to organize and manage the process. Life for Sally Windmuller was by no means easy — start-ups never are. But the early growth of the company as a technology-based business relied on a steady stream of product and process innovations which helped create value in the marketplace. This strength was deeply embedded so that even after the huge setbacks of both wars the company was able to emerge resurgent, riding an innovation wave.

But increasing growth in the automobile industry also brought new challenges to this innovation model. Demand for a wider range of products and more customized solutions sat alongside pressures to cut costs and delivery times whilst maintain a high quality standard. Close links with key vehicle makers tied Hella tightly to their tight and demanding development cycles. Overall, there was growing pressure on Hella's product and process engineers to do more with less as profit margins shrank.

Hella's response was multi-stranded. It invested heavily in pushing its technological frontiers, stretching to deliver novel lighting solutions. On the product innovation side, for example, Hella achieved a number of world 'firsts'. In 1991 they showed the xenon headlamp at the International Auto Exhibition in Frankfurt. This novel design effectively doubled the light output compared with conventional halogen headlights and cut the energy consumed by the lamp by one-third. Mass production of the xenon headlights for BMW began a year later, setting a trend in the industry, and Hella developed different variants over the next years including a headlamp system with both a high and a low beam. Although more expensive than halogen lamps, xenon lamps significantly increased a driver's field of vision at night.

The link to *process* innovation also became tighter. In order to lower development and production cost for the growing variety of car models — each with a distinctly different headlight design — Hella's engineers came up with a modular system based on tiny light emitting diodes. This LED-technology allowed the combination of pre-produced light modules in an unlimited number of variations. First introduced in 1992 for brake lights in a BMW convertible, the modular system was soon also used in other rear lights.

And Hella began to spread the range of application of these technologies, moving across into adjacent markets like commercial vehicles and trailers, motorcycles, bicycles, boats and trains. In 1996, the company spun off Hella Aerospace GmbH as an independent subsidiary for aviation lighting, which was later sold to Goodrich Corporation in the United States.

It was also during this time that electronics began to play an increasingly important role as a division in its own right, not just supplying controls for lighting systems but extending across a wide range of switches and relays, remote controls, electronic controls and sensors.

We'll explore several of these cases in more detail in the following chapter.

OPENING UP THEIR INNOVATION GAME

During the 1990s Hella also began to recognize a principle, common now in the era of 'open innovation' that *not all the smart guys work for us*. Trying to compete along such a complex technological frontier required developing networks and partnerships, and so Hella began to put these in place via a mixture of acquisitions, mergers and joint ventures. This view was particularly championed by Jürgen Behrend, who pioneered the 'network strategy' which helped fuel knowledge-led growth across the business.

Behrend also saw the company's future in intelligent automotive *systems* developed, manufactured and marketed by a network of independent suppliers such as Hella. This move anticipated what was to become an increasingly important shift in the role of automotive suppliers, moving from being simply shops where components could be purchased towards players with strategic knowledge and capability to put together whole systems.

Beginning in 1992, a new Hella plant in eastern Germany put out whole front-end modules for a number of Volkswagen models. In 1999, Hella established a joint venture with the German Behr group, a supplier of air conditioning and motor cooling units and a long-standing business partner. And in 2001, Hella entered two strategic partnerships that resulted in new joint ventures: one with Japanese lighting components manufacturer Stanley Electric and one with German automotive wiring specialist Leoni Bordnetz-Systeme. Two years later, Hella announced a strategic alliance with Japanese manufacturer Taiko Device Techno & Co. to jointly market automotive relays.

Today's elaboration of the network strategy involves strategic partnerships and joint ventures with dozens of companies supporting along the knowledge frontier and feeding into lighting, electronics, aftermarket and special applications fields. A good example is the current ability to work in the strategically important field of camera-based driver-assistance systems. Hella's ability to work in this space comes from their acquisition in 2006 of AGLAIA, a Berlin-based specialist for visual sensor systems.

Hella had always an 'after-market' business supplying replacements and spares to third party wholesalers, workshops and garages. During the early years of the 21st Century Hella's core lighting business was in crisis, making losses in 2003. Fortunately the after-market business remained strong and to reinforce this area, Hella introduced the 'Hella Service Partner' system aimed at building strong loyalty to the company among German car repair shops. And another key partnership was the joint venture Behr Hella Service which was established in 2005 to support the global independent after-market for vehicle air conditioning and engine cooling.

PROCESS INNOVATION — BIRTH OF THE HELLA PRODUCTION SYSTEM

Hella had ridden well on the coat-tails of expansion in the automobile industry during the 1980s but things became much tougher in the following decade. In particular, global competition was exposing big differences in productivity with Japanese manufacturers far ahead of the rest on a variety of key performance indicators. This began the search for process innovation which led to understanding the principles behind the 'lean' approach embodied in things like the Toyota Production System.

At its heart was a relentless attack on waste and a constant drive towards improved quality and productivity. This was achieved in part through high levels of employee involvement.

For the automotive supplier industry this signalled less a wake-up call than a full-scale alarm. The 'Lopez era' as it came to be known (named after the combative Purchasing Director of General Motors, Ignacio Lopez) challenged suppliers to make major improvements in cost, quality and delivery or cease trading with the major car-makers. As Dr Behrend pointed out at the time, for Hella it was a simple question — *'to be or not to be'*!

Central to the company's way forward was continuous improvement (CI) — finding ways to engage employees in the process of sustained incremental innovation. This wasn't just a new management technique but a fundamental shift in the underlying mental model which frames what the organization does — a 'paradigm innovation'. But in many ways it also harked back to one of the core values — 'entrepreneurial responsibility'.

But making CI happen involves more than just waving a flag and expecting people to rally behind it. If we are serious about CI then we need to create the conditions in which it can flourish — a culture in which CI is 'the way we do things around here'. And that depends on developing people and the organization in which they work. The core value in such a culture — and one which has been with Hella from its earliest days — is 'entrepreneurial responsibility'. It's a two-way thing — from the employees there is the expectation that they will deliver their creativity and energy towards continuous improvement and from the management side, that they will create the conditions within which people can feel fulfilled, supported, are given a sense of purpose and the opportunity to make their contribution.

Central to this is the idea of seeing employees as competent and responsible partners — and trusting them to behave as such. It needs leaders who are prepared not only to share these values but also to 'walk the talk', creating conditions in which there is reliability and trustworthiness, information and transparency, communication and creativity. And it particularly requires a certain attitude towards mistakes — innovation involves risks and experiments and these may not always work.

For Hella in the 1990s this was a challenge and an opportunity; as Dr Behrend wrote in a report to the Board recommending CI:

> *If our employees are convinced that at HELLA these goals and guidelines can work together, then it is my belief that it will be a significant precondition for greater success for HELLA in the 90s. (12 March, 1991)*

CI was embodied in the Total Quality Management concept introduced in 1991, which built on three core principles:

- Customer satisfaction as a top target
- Employees to be empowered and able to guarantee customer satisfaction
- Entrepreneurial responsibility — the strategic guideline for processes and organizational structures to support this

It worked — and one measure of success was that it helped Hella survive and grow. At the end of 1980s there were 30,000 independent suppliers but 25 years later only 10% of them are left.

LOOKING TO THE INNOVATION HORIZON

Today's innovation environment for Hella has a touch of the *déjà vu* about it. Sally Windmuller might not find it so strange — looking around there is the sense of an industry at the early fluid stages of its development. There are powerful technological forces opening up huge new possibilities — driverless cars, energy efficiency delivered through novel fuels like electricity or hydrogen, low emissions and above all intelligence. Mobility in the future is likely to involve intelligent devices capable of sensing and acting in strategic fashion, all part of a highly connected world of the Internet of things.

On the market side there are huge social shifts changing the role which vehicles and mobility play, and people's expectations around that. Consumers are increasingly wanting the opposite of Henry Ford's offer — the era has moved in a 100 years from mass production to mass customization with increasing demands for tailoring and personalization to individual needs. Ownership models are being challenged by alternatives based on rentals and sharing — and, at the limit, people are challenging whether they need a vehicle at all.

And there are strong forces shaping what can be done — legislation and regulatory pressures on emissions, safety and sustainability are redrawing the pitch on which the competitive game of automotive manufacturing is being played.

As if that were not enough for anyone to wrestle with, the new environment has attracted a whole new set of players to the game. Computer companies like Apple, knowledge giants like Google, independent visionary entrepreneurs like Tesla are pushing ahead, reshaping the competitive landscape.

There's no doubt that there will be opportunities in this new landscape — the question is how well Hella is positioned to seize them. Its success so far owes much to strategic management of the three core elements we mentioned at the start of the book:

- *Competence* — building and managing the knowledge base,

- *Capability* — being able to create value from the knowledge base, to translate ideas into innovations. And being able to repeat the trick by learning and embedding key lessons about how to make innovation happen,

- *Continuity* — finding ways of ensuring carryover of the innovation essence of the company, understanding and transmitting its DNA to future generations

Let's pause and look more closely in the next chapter at how this plays out, looking at some more detailed examples from Hella's innovation history.

FURTHER RESOURCES

You can find a number of useful resources — case studies, video and audio, and tools to explore some of the themes discussed in this chapter at www.innovation-portal.info

In particular:

- Case studies of company histories including Marshalls, 3M and Corning

- Case studies of the early motor industry, especially around the Model T Ford and its revolutionary influence on product and process innovation

REFLECTION QUESTIONS

1. Innovation is about change — but simply changing things randomly and in different directions is not likely to move the organization forward. As the old saying has it, 'if you don't know where you are going, you'll probably end up somewhere else!' So we need an innovation strategy, some kind of roadmap for guiding and shaping change and making sure we spend our limited resources as wisely as we can. Choose an organization and try to research their underlying strategy. What was the original 'big idea' they were trying to exploit when they began and what is their approach today? What are the major directions of change they are trying to use to move them forwards?

2. Find another example of a company history and compare its experiences with that of Hella; in particular, exploring how they rode out waves of external change in the political, technological, market and competitive spheres.

3. Choose a sector and try to explore it in terms of the following questions (you could use the examples of the lighting, imaging or music industry from the Innovation Portal).

o To what extent are the changes involved competence-enhancing (i.e. building on what a player in the industry already knows so they can strengthen their position) or competence destroying (i.e. something completely new which requires learning some new tricks) innovations?

o And for whom? (Think about the different players in the industry — who are the likely winners and losers).

o What strategies might a firm use to exploit the opportunities? (Again, think about the different players in the industry and how they might defend their positions or open up new opportunities).

NOTES

1. Much of this chapter is based on interviews and on a detailed history of Hella published by the company to mark its 100th anniversary in 1999.

2. For a detailed description of the early days of the automobile industry see Altschuler, Roos, Jones, and Womack (1984).

3

PATTERNS OF INNOVATION

HELLA'S INNOVATION HISTORY

Louis Pasteur, the famous French chemist is reputed to have said that *'chance favours the prepared mind'* — and that's still a valuable reminder of the importance of taking a strategic approach to innovation. Organizations don't survive to celebrate their 100th birthday just by being lucky — they make their own luck. Hella's ability to survive crises and ride out waves of opportunity owes a lot to being prepared in Pasteur's sense. Its investments have been in competence (building and nurturing a deep knowledge base), capability (learning how to turn that knowledge into value through establishing processes and structures to support innovation) and continuity (carrying the core values of the company forward, creating a culture of entrepreneurial responsibility).

Technology matters, of course, and Hella's innovation story is very much built on a foundation of respect for, and investment in, scientific knowledge. Acquiring the people who carry that knowledge, developing the skills to utilize it, adapting and configuring it to the point where it can be reused and reapplied across a platform or product offerings — these are very much the way Hella has learned to work. And underpinning this is a respect for the value of such knowledge — from Sally Windmuller's early recognition of the importance of investing in R&D, through the understanding brought by the Hueck and Röpke families as scientists and engineers, to the present day in which around a fifth of the company's employee base are working in some form of research and development.

Importantly, this is not just theoretical knowledge. Ever since Sally Windmuller began driving his own car through the streets of Lippstadt there have been opportunities for learning by doing, by experimenting, by prototyping. Many of the breakthrough innovations were not direct from the drawing board but the result of various pilot efforts — they didn't always work but all of them contributed to a deep 'hand-on' understanding of the underlying technology and what it could do.

And it's not simply in the field of products and processes that Hella has applied these principles. The early moves to becoming international in approach owed much to the same prototyping spirit — jumping in the water and learning to swim fast! Experimenting with new organization structures and methods to meet the proliferating challenges of the outside world, developing rich external knowledge networks through joint ventures and strategic collaborations, setting up specialist exploration capacity to provide early warning of key disruptive trends in the future.

All of this represents the outcome of a strategic approach married to entrepreneurial capability spread throughout the organization. Importantly, it's not just concentrated in the product area; as we'll see, Hella has been making a good job of extensively exploring its innovation space.

EXPLORING INNOVATION SPACE — THE 4PS FRAMEWORK

No organization has unlimited resources and so developing an innovation strategy needs to answer two key questions:

- Where could we innovate?

- Out of all the things we could do, which ones will we do, and why?

Navigators and map-makers use an essential tool (even in these days of GPS devices) — the compass. It gives them an idea of where they are and which direction to go in — and it's the same with innovation. In similar fashion we need some way of mapping possible directions for innovation and to help us put the resources and energy behind getting us there.

To begin with we can think about four different directions in which innovation can happen. We can change:

- The product or service — what we offer the world

- The process — the way we create and deliver that offering

- The position — who we offer it to and the story we tell about it

- The paradigm or business model — the way we think about what our organization does and who we do it for

This '4P's framework' gives us an idea of the 'innovation space' we have for our organization and helps us answer the question 'where could we innovate?' It's also important to recognize that there is a spectrum along each of these dimensions, running from simple incremental improvement ('doing what we do a little better') right through to something the world may never have seen before ('doing something radically different') (**Figure 3.1**).[1]

For any organization there's plenty of innovation space and we can think of a number of journeys we could take, not just along the four main directions but in combinations. For example, we could do what Nintendo did with the Wii and the DS — introduce a new product which also allowed them to open up a new market — people who had never played computer games before. Or we could do what McDonalds did, opening up the market for fast food by learning lessons from Henry Ford's mass production process innovation in car making.

Figure 3.1. A Map of Innovation Space.

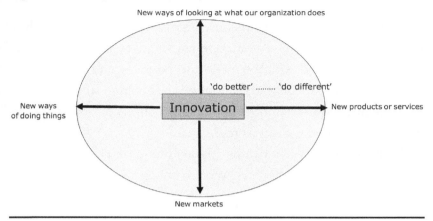

Table 3.1 gives some examples mapped on to the 4Ps.

EXPLORING HELLA'S INNOVATION SPACE

So how does this apply to Hella and the development of its innovation? Let's look at each of the main directions in a little more detail.

Product Innovation

This has always been at the heart of Hella's business and, as we've seen, extensive investment in R&D has meant a string of 'firsts' plus a systematic consolidation around incremental improvement in quality, cost and customization.

Hella's commitment to this has enabled a steady stream of product innovations, often being the first to introduce new categories. For example:

- the idea of halogen headlamps had been around since the 1960s and Hella began its work in 1962; by 1971 it was able to supply VW with the first production model in Germany.

Table 3.1. Some Examples.

Innovation	Where It Fits on the Model	Explanation
1. Haagen Dazs ice cream	Incremental position innovation	Opened up new market space by redefining ice cream as something which adults could enjoy.
2. 'Power by the hour' business model for Rolls Royce and General Electric aero engine business	Incremental paradigm — business model — innovation	Essentially redefined the business as being about service and support rather than products.
3. i-Pod player	Incremental product innovation	The player itself is simply a well-designed hard disk storage drive with playback features. Apple didn't invent the concept but did produce a very popular improvement on the original.
4. i-Tunes	Radical paradigm — business model — innovation	Fundamentally changes the way an increasingly large number of people buy and use music — allowed customization, cost reduction, increased access to a wider range of artists, etc. Apple had to work hard to put all the pieces of the puzzle in place — managing copyright, distribution, etc.
5. Toyota production system	Radical process innovation	Fundamentally changed the approach which car makers (and later many other industries) used to build cars. Placed much greater emphasis on team working, on reduced waste and on 'just-in-time' pull systems rather than trying to forecast demand and holding large inventories 'just-in-case'.
6. Outsourcing IT services	Incremental process innovation	Essentially the shift here is to move the delivery of services to a different firm — but the same operations are carried out. The analogy with a laundry service is relevant here — it is easier for some people to have this done for them by an outside agency.
7. Airbus A319	Incremental product innovation	Although containing some interesting technical enhancements and targeted at a particular need in the aviation market this is basically a variation on an established wide bodied, 2-engine jet theme.

Table 3.1. (*Continued*)

Innovation	Where It Fits on the Model	Explanation
8. Bausch and Lomb's 'eye wear' to 'eye care' business model shift (getting out of selling glasses, contact lenses, etc. and into high-tech fields like laser surgery equipment)	Incremental paradigm — business model — innovation	Although there is a redefining of the business away from low value commodity items like disposable contact lenses the underlying business still is about eyes and uses the deep understanding of this business which the company has built up over nearly a century.
9. Supermarket shopping	Radical process innovation	When the supermarket concept was first developed in the United States and later imported into Europe in the 1950s it fundamentally changed the way we think about the retail process — away from service by shop assistants and towards self-service.
10. Low cost airlines	Radical position innovation	Essentially took the concept of flying and made it available to a new set of users who previously couldn't participate because the costs were too high. This lowering of the price meant that a whole new market was created rather than simply segmenting an existing one.
11. Voice over Internet Protocol (VOIP) telephony	Radical process innovation	Fundamental change in the way telephone calls are made, from using fixed lines or mobile (cellular) to running it via the Internet. In changing the model there have been radical drops in the costs and many providers like Skype are offering an element of completely free calling.
12. 'Capsule' hotels — very small rooms (originally developed in Japan) with basic facilities for city centre overnight stays	Incremental product innovation	Essentially an interesting variant on the basic theme of a hotel room — in this case addressing a particular need for low cost city centre accommodation.

13. Low cost 'single serving' shampoo sachets for the Indian market targeted at low income (<$2/day) households	Incremental position innovation	Essentially opens up a new market segment amongst the very poor in countries like India — this group would like quality shampoo but cannot afford the 'normal' 250 ml size bottle.
14. Henry Ford's mass production factory	Radical paradigm — business model — innovation	Although the elements were developed in many earlier industries Ford's engineers brought together technologies and working practices to standardize both product and process and massively reduce the costs of making a product — in this case the 'car for Everyman' at a price Everyman could afford. The mass production model spread to most manufacturing and many service sectors from the 1920s onwards.
15. Screw-top wine closures	Incremental product innovation	Although this substitution of screw caps for corks has had an impact on the cork industry it has been a relatively minor improvement in the wider wine business.
16. Online banking and insurance	Radical process innovation	Fundamentally changed the way in which financial and other services were delivered, moving from face-to-face delivery which was labour-intensive to a much more automated and lower cost process.
17. Penicillin and other antibiotics	Radical product innovation	Opened up a completely new field in pharmaceutical industry.
18. Flat beds on transatlantic business class airline routes	Incremental product innovation	Improvement in service as a result of relatively minor changes to the physical seating and cabin arrangements.
19. White LED lighting	Radical product innovation	Fundamental shift in the price and performance with high levels of energy efficiency (85% better) and longer life (×20).
20. Online health advice — for example, NHS Direct in the UK	Incremental process innovation	Offering health advice service via online or telephone as opposed to face-to-face with a doctor or nurse.

This table lists some examples of innovation of different kinds mapped on to the compass.

- similarly its investment in lamp geometry meant it could launch a 'free form' technology based on early applications of computer-aided design. This began in 1988 and quickly became the industry standard as key customers began to expect the ability to shape lights to fit in with exciting new body styles.

- in 1991 a Mercedes car fitted with a radical new technology — Xenon discharge lamps — was shown at the Frankfurt Motor show and once again established Hella's reputation for innovation.

- 1992 also saw the first application of solid state lighting — LEDs — in a brake light set for BMW Series 3. This was once again a radical innovation for the sector but underpinned by a significant investment in learning by Hella.

- 1994 saw another key step — the integration of multiple lighting systems into a common network linked by a fibre optic cable. CELIS — Central Lighting Systems — mapped out a future road trajectory along which vehicle electronics would increasingly be connected and controlled in an integrated system rather than as isolated components.

It wasn't just lighting technologies — other fields were developed in similar entrepreneurial fashion. For example the concept of climate control was pioneered in the company and through an early partnership with Porsche. Bodywork electronics — embedding intelligence and control in the car (e.g. in seats) — became another area of expertise.

(And it's worth remembering that through all of this the company were still making — and innovating — the horns with which the business had begun a century earlier!)

The long tradition of product innovation has been accompanied by an important shift away from simple component-level solutions to offering systems and moving towards platform architectures. Approaches like these provide a powerful competitive edge since they require assembling different elements of knowledge into a higher-level framework (we'll discuss this theme in more detail in Chapter 9 but for now it is worth noting that while this has become a key plank in Hella's innovation strategy it is also something with a long history). Right back in the early days of headlights the Hella system, linking light source, lens and reflector, was an example of an architectural innovation. And later work with electronics benefitted hugely from the integration of hardware and software knowledge and key application domains; success stories like climate control have their roots in this approach.

A danger facing many technology-based companies is that their innovation model becomes too much one of 'knowledge push', creating products which appear to their designers to be exciting but for which there is no real market demand. To some extent this characterized the approach to product innovation in electronics in the early 1990s but it was replaced by a model that brought a much stronger element of market communication with it. Through product management the needs of particular customers could be used as a key input to the product development process.

This model persists with a growing understanding of the importance of understanding not just direct customers like car manufacturers but in constructing end-user cases which see potential Hella product ideas applied in the context of people's lives, helping with mobility, security and other aspects. Importantly, the process has shifted, in part reflecting Hella's deep technological competence, to one of 'co-creation' where new ideas are jointly conceived and explored by Hella and its key customers. 'Consultative marketing' of this kind is increasingly being used as a way of bringing stakeholders around a table to explore jointly what might be done using Hella's technology to meet emerging needs. Given the growing emphasis on intelligent devices — the 'Internet of things' — this approach to product innovation is likely to be increasingly important.

Process Innovation — Rethinking How Hella Operates

Innovation is not only about new products and services but also about changes in the ways we create and deliver those offerings. From its earliest days Hella had to work at finding new and efficient ways to produce in increasing volumes and one of their earliest moves was into learning the techniques of mass production back in the 1920s. Its subsequent development involved consistent investment in learning around new techniques — for example, working with plastics and, in the 1960s, moving into the very different field of electronics, mastering not only the core technologies but how to integrate them with mechanical components and assemble complete systems.

Process innovation is not just about machinery and equipment; it is also about the way the organization works and the underlying philosophy of production. During the 1980s Europe saw the beginnings of a radical change in its approaches as the implications of the 'total quality management' approach began to emerge. The lessons from successful Japanese manufacturers — especially those in the automobile industry — had shown the importance of quality and its management on a systematic basis. Total quality management was supported by challenging frameworks based around ISO 9000 and Hella moved into achieving these in the early 1990s, along with a major rethink of the whole approach to manufacturing.[2] The principles of 'lean' thinking began to be absorbed, experimented with and deployed in Hella's own style and led to the rollout around the world of the 'Hella Production system'. (We'll look at this in more detail in the following chapter.)

Another key element in process innovation concerns the close networking between suppliers and final producers, and in the automobile industry this has been a key area for change. From its early days building close links with VW Hella has worked to partner with major manufacturers streamlining logistics and even locating satellite production facilities on the sites of final assemblers. Coupled with techniques like modular design — for example, supplying an entire front-end assembly for VW with headlamps, indicators and other elements already built in — such process innovation contributes to continuous improvements around cost, delivery time and quality.

Process innovation isn't just about plant, equipment and physical processes. Innovation can only take place if there is a foundation within the organization of people willing and able to support change. And this requires a commitment to their recruitment, development and retention. From its earliest days Hella has been committed to these values, seeing its skilled and experienced staff as a key resource in growing an entrepreneurial business. It has invested in education and training since its pioneering role in establishing apprenticeships back in the 1920s and this tradition persists; for example, Hella played a major role in helping establish a Fachhochschule (technical university) in the city of Lippstadt in 2014. And, except for the very dark days of the 1930s recession, the company has maintained a policy of avoiding redundancies wherever possible.

At its heart is a core value which the company expresses as 'entrepreneurial responsibility'. Essentially, this means a simultaneous expectation placed on all employees to contribute their ideas, energy and creativity to help the business grow, and on the part of management to ensure that the conditions which enable that to happen are present. This is the critical element; for such an approach to work there needs to be clear strategic leadership and direction coupled to investment to demonstrate real commitment to those principles.

One example that illustrates this is the long-running employee suggestion scheme, which draws out ideas from across the workforce for improvements in products and processes with which they work. More recent has been the use of an innovation contest — 'Driving e-nnovation' — to challenge and inspire employees to work together on novel and entrepreneurial ideas.

Another part of the challenge in a growing organization is the willingness to rethink and challenge the existing structures for innovation. It's easy when the business is a small entrepreneurial unit; people share common vision and are very clear what the strategic targets are to survive and grow. But as the business becomes more successful so it starts to specialize, bringing in more people and organizing them into different specialist groups. This process inevitably raises challenges around co-ordinating and integrating all the different specialist sources of knowledge and requires a rethink about how the organization should be structured and operate.

This crisis came for Hella in the early 1990s. As the organization had grown and become more specialized so barriers between different areas emerged and, in particular, there was a separation between the R&D/design activities and the manufacturing world. With the help of external consultants a new model was introduced in 1993, which offered a more closely integrated structure supporting innovation right from initial idea generation through to large-scale manufacturing. This reduced the time to market for new ideas and enhanced their quality by bringing in shared perspectives and avoiding unnecessary duplication of resources.

This kind of organizational innovation highlights the need to develop complementary but parallel capabilities to address an increasingly complex environment. Hella's journey began with a simple ad hoc structure, moved through various kinds of formalization and specialization and, by the time of its 100th birthday, was facing challenges along a broad front, ranging from working in many different international markets, through dealing with increasingly complex technologies and systems, to finding ways to work with markets composed not only of traditional players but also new entrants and disruptive forces. To expect a single innovation organization to handle all these challenges is clearly unrealistic and Hella's recent moves have been to create and foster parallel activities to support its innovation strategy.

Position Innovation — Moving into New Markets

Innovation isn't just about products — it's also about where we place them. We can innovate by changing the context — moving to new market segments or shifting the geographical base. For a firm of its size Hella was quick to explore and set up in other locations and to commit to more than just a sales office. And this was not just a case of following the key players; Hella opened a factory in Australia in 1961 anticipating the move there by VW. It followed this with other early and important strategic licence arrangements with Brazil and India, paving the way for its international footprint.

Importantly, moving into new markets isn't simply about expansion of demand. There is also a huge learning opportunity, working in different contexts and with different users to meet their needs. Position innovation of this kind can be a powerful *source* of innovation, although making these moves was a mixture of experiment and strategy, and the early steps weren't always successful. But by the 1970s the company was able to take a much more organized and systematic approach to internationalization, building on lessons learned about how to manage and consolidate their network.

It's possible to see four waves of internationalization carried through with increasing degrees of 'professionalization':

- Wave 1 was essentially entrepreneurially led, with target countries selected largely through personal connections or because of key customer pull. Moves into Australia, the United States and Brazil fit into this category.

- Wave 2 was driven more by a deliberate attempt to extend the footprint and was very much led by the lighting division. They were associated with changing production costs and availability of skills as well as proximity to new markets. Moves here were also with strategic partners and joint ventures.

- Wave 3 extended into further strategically rising regions especially China and India.

- Wave 4 consolidated these with a growing number of joint ventures, especially in China.

Similarly during its expansion Hella began looking for new
markets in which to deploy its growing knowledge base — working in aircraft, marine, agricultural and a wide range of other
sectors adjacent to its core automotive business.

And an important element of Hella's business had always been
the after-market — supplying replacements and spare parts to the
service and workshop trade. Finding new ways of working with
this market, developing a deeper understanding of its segments
and their specific needs was an important feed into the innovation
strategy. Not least the increasingly high technological component
in such services meant that this market began to demand its own
supporting products and services. A good example is the field of
diagnostics; with the rise in electronics in vehicles since the 1980s
has come a revolution in the way their performance can be moni-
tored and problems quickly found and fixed. Diagnostic equipment came to form a key part of Hella's product offering and led
to several strategic alliances and joint ventures, including the
establishment of Hella Gutmann as a major player in this sector.
Importantly the knowledge gained from working with these
specialized markets provides a powerful feedback channel to the
mainstream new product development system as well.

Importantly, innovation strategy is about pushing frontiers and
exploring radically new territory. One attempt to move in this
direction was the setting up of a new division with the remit to
explore nonautomotive applications of Hella's knowledge base.
Hella Industries faced an uphill struggle, simultaneously trying to
learn about very different markets (and their underlying dynamics)
and adapt their technologies to very different kinds of products.
This moved them into fields like street lighting systems and

industrial lighting applications and also to explore innovative arrangements to finance these and share risks.

In the event this proved difficult and took attention from the core challenges of growing the mainstream business. It had been a valuable learning process and laid the foundations for what might in the future be re-entry into some of the markets explored but in 2016 the division was sold off.

Position innovation is also concerned with the business-to-business world — internal markets along a supply chain. An important direction for innovation here concerns the role which an organization can create for itself within a wider system. Much is made these days about the idea of platforms and examples like Intel are instructive; they build a strong position by becoming the central point around which many players orbit. Suppliers of components design them to link to Intel processors; manufacturers of computers, phones, etc., design with 'Intel inside' in mind, and consumers recognize the underlying reliability of such an architecture. Intel has effectively positioned itself at the heart of a platform business model.

In similar fashion Hella has increasingly become a key player, linking the worlds of technology suppliers such as semiconductor makers with those of downstream customers like the car manufacturers. Building and sustaining those knowledge networks places Hella in a strong position, gaining knowledge about technology and market trends from both sides of this relationship and using this to ensure their continued central role in future developments.

Position innovation is not just about markets. It is also about the story an organization tells to its markets, how it positions itself in the minds of its customers. In Hella's case this has always been a message about technological competence and innovation but in recent years the storytelling has become more strategic. Hella is a valuable partner with whom it becomes possible to explore new frontiers — an organization with whom shared risk-taking can take place. This has a long history in the company — for example the early development of xenon lighting or climate control systems both began with an approach by a carmaker looking to explore new territory.

The extent to which this is happening can be gauged by a presentation made to a major industry marketing event — the 2015 Frankfurt Auto Show IAA — at which Hella set out their approach:

> *This year our IAA motto is 'making sense(s)'. We think that the connected vehicle requires additional senses, such as sense of touch, smell and sight to allow the integration of the vehicle into a digital network of 'mobility units …'.*
>
> *(w)e provide connected vehicles with (human) senses that allow interpretation and interaction with the environment … this is how innovative technology can make our life easier.*

A long way from smoky acetylene lamps — but the connections are still clear to see.

'Paradigm Innovation' — Rethinking the Business Model

Occasionally organizations need to think about innovation not just in what they do — products, markets, processes — but also in who they are. What is the underlying business model, how does innovation create value in their market place? Such change happens less frequently but is a powerful source of disruption since it is often by rethinking the business model that entrepreneurs can gain a foothold. Think about Über, AirBnB or the low cost airlines — all of them revolutionized industries without changing the core technology of products or processes. Instead they rethought the ways in which those businesses could operate.

Paradigm innovation — borrowing the Greek word for 'world view' — is important to an organization like Hella since many of the external shifts in both the technological and social/market environment may mean that the core model that has served them well needs to change. For example, there is a strong and growing trend in manufacturing towards 'servitization' — wrapping services around core products and building long-term relationships with customers who buy — or more often rent — the overall service. Aircraft engine makers like Rolls-Royce and GE now offer 'power by the hour' to their customers, while equipment makers like Caterpillar are rebuilding their business based on a similar model where customers pay for the usable hours their equipment provides. This forces manufacturers to rethink their product designs and their support and maintenance arrangements as well as selling their core proposition.[3]

Another paradigm innovation has been the shift towards 'open innovation'. Innovation is all about creating value from ideas. So it makes sense for companies to invest in ways of building up its knowledge base — doing R&D of various kinds. But in a world where there is so much knowledge creation going on — we don't know exactly but estimates suggest as much as €16 billion is spent every year around the world on R&D — the game is changing. Even the largest organization has to recognize that 'not all the smart people work for us ...'. And as soon as you say that, everything changes. The innovation engine becomes one of knowledge flow, knowledge trading, enabling ideas to move around much more freely.[4]

The idea behind this isn't new — it's been at the heart of innovation for centuries. But it was an influential article and book published by U.S. professor Henry Chesbrough in 2003 which gave us the label 'open innovation', describing the challenge posed by learning to work in this world where owning knowledge is no longer as important as trading it. Procter and Gamble were one of the early explorers of this concept, changing their 150-year-old innovation model of R&D-based knowledge production and exploitation to a new approach — 'Connect and develop' which saw them trying to source half of their new ideas from outside the company.

Open innovation offers some attractive opportunities. Instead of having to do all the hard work alone organizations like Hella can leverage the knowledge of others. And there may be many cases where Hella knowledge is underutilized in the core business but where it could usefully be deployed by someone else. The challenge is working out how to move from the idea to the reality? How do we find partners outside the organization and work with them? What knowledge do we have that someone else might benefit from and how can we manage those relationships?

Open innovation has undoubtedly changed the innovation landscape over the past 20 years — but it is not a new idea. And Hella has been working with these principles for a long time, just not labelling it 'open innovation'. Back in the 1990s one of Jürgen Behrend's strategic interventions was to move the company towards a networked model, seeking strategic alliances and joint ventures in order to be able to play an increasingly knowledge-intensive game effectively.

A good example is the acquisition of Hella Aglaia, a company which began life a long way from Hella's core world of automotive lighting. A small Hamburg-based start-up, Aglaia worked on innovative sensing and counting technologies linked to movements of people — for example, in retail outlets or busy stations. Their core vision and sensing technologies have become critical to the world in which Hella is now operating with driverless cars and other innovations dependent on advanced sensing tools and techniques. Since Hella's acquisition in 1998 the company has increased dramatically in size, relocating to Berlin and now employing over 250 people. The importance has been not just in its deep specialist knowledge base but also the networks which it carried with it, linking Hella to other key knowledge resources. And the business also offers a different lens through which Hella can explore its environment — for example, Aglaia are working on other mobility solutions such as mass transit railways — which may represent part of the very different future for transportation.

EXPLORING A NEW INNOVATION LANDSCAPE

So far, so good. Hella has a long and successful history of innovation and has managed to move from a small entrepreneurial business to become a global player, leader in many of the markets in which it works. But it can't afford to rest on its laurels — the big challenge in innovation is that it involves a constantly moving target.

The innovation environment today is richer than ever in terms of the opportunities it offers — and the challenges it poses. As we've seen, 'open innovation' has become a key theme, recognizing that in a world where so much new knowledge is being created we need new innovation approaches and structures that allow 'open innovation' to work.

At the same time the role of users in innovation is becoming increasingly significant. User innovators have always mattered but we are now in a world where technology enables us to access ideas from anyone — and to do so rapidly and in ways which can make a big contribution to shaping and configuring innovation so that they diffuse successfully. 'Crowd-sourcing' has moved from a few people sharing ideas to a powerful vehicle for making innovation happen — including providing the funding to support ideas; in an era of 'crowd-funding' everyone can be a business angel as well as an innovator!

Not all markets are shaped the same way — and with the huge growth in 'emerging markets' has come a realization of the need to rethink innovation approaches. Since many of those markets — not just Brazil, India or China but behind them Africa, the rest of Asia and Latin America — are made up of high volumes of people but with relatively low purchasing power there is a growing interest in 'frugal innovation'. What sorts of products and services could we offer which provide a good enough solution, a value proposition which works for those contexts? And — when something as complex as a car can be designed, built and sold for less than \$3,000 — what might this mean for more established markets that are now becoming more value conscious?

Perhaps the most dramatic shift in the landscape has come with the rethinking of many of the fundamental assumptions on which business models have been built — and the disruption that is bringing to many markets. Low cost airlines transformed the idea of short-haul flying, opening up the experience to millions of new customers but via an approach which fundamentally challenged existing players. Businesses like Uber and AirBnB have transformed traditional sectors, yet neither of them owns a single vehicle or property; instead they have rethought the underlying business model. This process of 'business model innovation' requires looking again at social, market, political, technological trends and seeing where value could be created in new ways. With a growing number of young people no longer interested in ownership of high cost assets like cars or houses what does this mean for business models based on a rental economy? With technological shifts enabling driverless cars what might this mean for the industry — both in terms of challenges to existing markets and opening up of new ones? And will it take new entrants like Apple and Google to innovate new business models because established players can't let go of their old ones?

We could go on listing features of the current innovation environment but the point is clear; organizations need to think hard about their approach to these and to be prepared to adapt and change their innovation strategies and processes to survive and grow.

How Hella has done this in the past and how it is facing up to the current challenges is a theme we pick up in the next section of the book. But before we look at these it is important to remind ourselves of how innovation takes place and the key role played by internal entrepreneurs in this.

FURTHER RESOURCES

You can find a number of useful resources — case studies, video and audio, and tools to explore some of the themes discussed in this chapter at www.innovation-portal.info

In particular:

- Case studies of organizations exploring open innovation — Procter and Gamble, Lego, Adidas, Threadless, Local Motors

- Case histories of other organizations showing their shifting innovation emphasis around the 4Ps space — Marshalls, 3M, Philips, Corning

- Video explanations of the 4Ps approach and of the challenge of working with 'knowledge spaghetti' in this open innovation context

REFLECTION QUESTIONS

1. Choose an organization and try to develop a competency map that highlights their core strengths in their knowledge base, and where and how they have used — and might use in the future — these competencies to create value through innovation. (You can find more background and a tool framework at www.innovation-portal.info)

2. Use the 4Ps approach to build a map of innovation space and how it is explored in an organization of your choosing.

3. Think of an organization and explore the underlying business model they use to create value. How has this changed over time — and how might it be changed in the future? In particular think about the following questions:

o How could you provide different ways of creating the core value proposition?

o Could you change/expand the target market segments?

o Which new/alternative channels might you use to reach them?

o Which new technologies might you take advantage of?

o Which new partners might you link with to improve the way value is delivered?

o How can you cut costs?

o How can you add or improve revenue streams?

NOTES

1. You can find more detail about the 4P approach and other tools for exploring innovation space in Joe Tidd and John Bessant (2014).

2. You can find more detail about the lean manufacturing revolution in Womack and Jones (2005).

3. For more about business model innovation see Osterwalder and Pigneur (2010) and Afuah (2003).

4. For more about open innovation see Chesbrough (2003) and Reichwald, Huff, and Moeslein (2013).

4

WE ARE THE CHAMPIONS

On the corner of the Rixbecker Strasse in Lippstadt there's a long, low-slung building with a big advertising poster stretching along its side. Not particularly exciting — but go through the entrance doors at one end and you are transported to a special kind of theatre. Stretching ahead of you is a road, half a kilometre long, thrusting its way into the distance. Token scenery helps give the effect of a straight piece of Germany along which you are driving. Turn out the lights — and a particular magic begins. With the help of clever simulation you can imagine yourself driving a 1930s VW, a Maybach from the 1950s or the latest Audi. More importantly, you get a vivid sense of how important the headlamps are, in terms of what you can see and when. You can move through the generations from yesterday's feeble yellow glow just about revealing the surface a few metres in front of you (1920s technology) to today's laser sharp LED beams opening up the road almost as brightly as in daylight. And you can even keep your full beam lights on in today's version — there is clever technology which cuts out the glare that your headlights would represent to an oncoming car.

Welcome to Hella's Lichtkanal (Light Channel). This isn't simply an excellent marketing show to demonstrate the wonders of Hella lighting technology — it's a key part of the R&D effort. Just as a wind tunnel gives aircraft designers important information about new airframe and wing designs so the Lichtkanal offers valuable feedback to Hella's team working on new lamp and lighting technologies.

It underlines their commitment to knowledge — to acquiring and managing it. As we explored in Chapter 1, accumulating and deploying your knowledge base — competence — is one of the key tasks in innovation strategy. It's not easy, and it doesn't come cheap — Hella spends nearly 10% of turnover on such activity and it has been doing so for a long time. But it does pay off — investments in building competence in the past are what have enabled Hella to play a successful game in the present.

COMPETENCE ISN'T ENOUGH

But competence is only part of the story — we also need the capacity to create value from that investment in ideas. Innovation *capability* is about building the structures, processes and policies that allow an organization to do so, and to repeat the trick. It's easy to think of this as simply process maps or structures on an organization chart — but the reality, of course, is that it is about people. They are the ones who effect the translation, turning knowledge into value. Structures and processes help but in the end it is the ways in which people behave that make things happen.

And that's where the 'entrepreneur' comes in — the change agent, the person or team who enable innovation. Providing the bridge between good ideas and their ability to create value, alchemists can transmute base metals into gold. It's not magic or black art but a set of skills and characteristics, a pattern of behaviour which involves seeing possibilities, experimenting, learning, exploring and testing — and all driven by passion and energy (**Figure 4.1**).

We've become accustomed to one picture of entrepreneurs — the pioneering hero/heroine who takes on the world and starts something new. Steve Jobs, Anita Roddick, Bill Gates, Elon Musk,

Figure 4.1. The Key Role of Entrepreneurs.

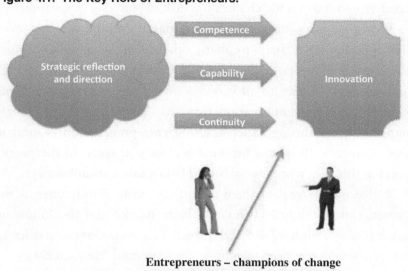

Entrepreneurs – champions of change

Jeff Bezos — there's a long list of examples. But the reality is that innovation is not a solo act, it's very much a team game and most entrepreneurship takes place through the efforts of multiple players. Apple wove a nice PR story round Steve Jobs but their success owed a great deal to the skills and drive of others like Jonathan Ive who helped realize his ideas. Pixar's reputation for consistent innovation wasn't built on a lone genius but on a culture of creative teamworking. Great innovators like Thomas Edison understood this — his business was not based on his genius but on the team which he carefully assembled and led in his 'invention factory'.

Innovation is what entrepreneurs do — and a great deal of it happens on a less heroic scale and an everyday basis. Within organizations it is people who carry new ideas forward, connect them with others, drive, persuade, nudge and challenge to make something happen. Individual managers may be given a specific task around innovation — but as we know, the process is not like a simple machine in which pressing the 'start' button leads to an output.

Instead they need to bring their energy, ideas, networks, skills and creativity to bear on the challenging task of enabling innovation.[1]

We sometimes hear about 'internal entrepreneurs' or even 'intrapreneurs' but there are many other labels which also capture the essence of this role. 'Promoters', 'champions', 'change agents', 'gatekeepers' — they're all versions of the same idea, the internal players who carry innovation forward. Making effective change happen comes through such internal entrepreneurship — and in this chapter we'll look a little more closely at some of the people playing this role who have shaped Hella's innovation history.

We've met several of them already — Sally Windmuller at the outset, Oskar Eduard Hueck, Wilhelm Röpke and the following generations, Reinhard Röpke, Jürgen Behrend. Characteristics of all of them have been classic entrepreneurial characteristics — energy, enthusiasm, vision and a willingness to experiment and take risks. But Hella's success isn't just a result of their efforts; it comes about through the context which they helped create, one in which many other entrepreneurial managers have been able to make a contribution. The principle of 'entrepreneurial responsibility' particularly articulated by Jürgen Behrend is at the heart of Hella's innovation DNA — the expectation that each employee will contribute to the innovation story and the responsibility of senior leaders to create the conditions in which they can.

MILESTONES OF INNOVATION

To illustrate how this operates we'll look at some key innovation milestones in Hella's history and explore the way in which internal entrepreneurs — champions/promoters/change agents — have played a key role. These are only a handful but they serve to underline the importance of this approach to managing innovation:

— Building electronics into Hella's DNA

— Pioneering new applications like climate control

- Lighting the way forward — Xenon, LED and future generations

- Rethinking the Hella production system

- Creating the innovation engine for the future

This isn't just about history — looking back. We can see the same thing today, looking out across the present Hella world there are similar champions at work moving forward with frugal, agile, disruptive innovation. We'll look more closely at them in the next section of the book.

Building Electronics into Hella's DNA

Hella began life making accessories, in particular lights. But from the 1960s something else began to grow which was to have huge significance for the company's later development. Electronics — and with it the possibilities of putting increasing levels of intelligent control into the accessories — began to play a part. For a company like Siemens or Bosch with a long history in the electrical/electronics world this was a logical extension of their activity. But for Hella this was a move unto unknown territory and one which challenged them on several fronts. The complexity of learning about a new technological field, the difficulty of finding suitably skilled staff, the change in approach in areas like design — this was a whole new and very strange world.

Hella entered not by accident but as a result of strategic commitment — this is the competence building thread we talked about in Chapter 1. And the investment paid off; from its tiny beginnings in the 1960s, the electronics division (GE — Geschäftsbereich Elektronik) has become a major cornerstone of the company, with a growing role as a preferred partner for key customers. Hella GE is positioned less as a 'me too' supplier and more of a technological leader, co-creating opportunities with key customers who see where and how electronics can be used, and working with key suppliers like semiconductor manufacturers to make sure they remain ahead of the technological curve.

Of course the industry is changing — but in this case the challenge has been one that is pushing the car industry towards exploring very new territory. Not for nothing are offices springing up all over Silicon Valley — this new gold rush reflects just how important electronics has become. Whatever the nature of the mobility solution and whoever owns or drives the vehicle in the future there is a very good chance that the software and hardware around making it intelligent will be critical.

It's taken 50 years to mature but Hella's strong position reflects our idea of internal champions, entrepreneurs working within the system to help create value from the investments in technological competence. For example, Karl-Heinz Krücken who joined the company in 1967 with a background in precision engineering; he was originally part of a small concept exploration group and built up his speciality around measurement. Amongst other things he became a plastics expert, knowledgeable around blow and other moulding techniques; when Hella sold off its plastics interests he moved to work on special projects which eventually became the Advanced Engineering group. Here, he worked extensively on early generation electronic products like the speed regulator.

Or Friedrich Waldeyer, who joined around the same time, bringing his mechanical engineering skills to the team.

And Christian Trowitsch, an electronics engineer who spent his early career in the field of colour television design and manufacture during the late 1960s. He played a key role in creating a specialist electronics capability during the 1980s, growing it from nothing to over 180 people before he retired in 2002.

THE LONG ROAD FROM BLINKERS TO BODY
CONTROL MODULES — AND BEYOND

Hella had begun to experiment with simple electronics in the 1960s and launched a blinking turn indicator device in 1967. But electronics was very much an add-on component level thing; the big shift came as the technology moved from stand-alone and simple integrated circuits to increasingly high levels of integration on a single chip. And with the development of the microprocessor in 1971 came the increasingly important contribution of software and programmability.

By the 1980s the auto industry had begun to recognize the significant potential of electronics and there was an acceleration towards their widespread adoption to improve comfort, safety, emissions and security. Possibilities were also opening up for electronic diagnosis and for the potential replacement of whole systems of mechanical components. All of this created strong demand from the customer side but also a big challenge for Hella; they needed to think carefully about the major strategic shift into this field.

In 1982 Hella's product range was essentially based around simple electronics — electro-mechanical equipment such as relays, horns, water pumps for windscreen wipers, vacuum pumps and various sensors. And they had a few software-driven applications, especially the speed regulator. It was clear that if they were going to ride this new wave in the industry they would need to expand and focus their competence.

The swing towards integrated electronics led to considerable expansion across Hella's workforce. But it was not simply expansion in numbers; there was also a big shift in the skills and content of work involved. This was especially apparent in the design area where the long traditions of mechanical design were being replaced by electronics and circuit design. And software became an increasingly important area. For each new product there was a need for a minimum of two software developers who could work on both hardware and software. But at the start this was precariously underpinned — only between 15 and 20 young engineers were available who had these skills and the external labour market was already empty. So Hella had no alternative but to train young people from scratch by recruiting straight from universities and technical colleges — a 'grow-your-own' philosophy. Even then they were competing with companies like Siemens and Bosch who could offer more attractive work packages and who had well-established recruiting processes.

The challenge was not just to find somewhere to work, it lay also in the ways in which these young staff worked. In fact, the organization structure helped enable a unified development process which was fast and bridged effectively across different functions. A lack of space and facilities meant that they were all working closely together and shared ideas and information quickly and easily. (There are echoes here of Lockheed's famous Skunk Works facility in the United States of America where a throng of breakthrough innovations emerged from a small team who were originally housed in an old circus tent because there was not space in the main factory for them.)[2]

Their ability to develop new products fast came from a number of causes. In particular the acute skills shortage forced new staff to learn both hardware and software — unlike in larger organizations where these functions would have been managed separately. The youngsters had no other choice than to learn to program the microprocessors which they were also designing into their new circuits. They had to work in machine code, whereas in larger firms (like Siemens or Bosch) the staff could work on high level languages running on PCs and then transport the software to the hardware. The Hella approach meant that development was parallel rather than serial and the idea of systems thinking became embedded early on.

For example, engineers would learn about software for injectors at the same time as understanding the motors involved. Or those working on climate control not only understood the programming side but also had a sense of the whole hardware system to deliver it. This gave a significant advantage in quickly translating customer needs and wishes into concrete examples. An approach born out of necessity became a powerful innovation advantage for the firm.

Another set of issues concerned the shift in design skills and technology. Hella was an early user of computer aided design (CAD) but most systems for this had evolved around the needs of mechanical design; the growing move to electronics required newer approaches. This shift was complicated by the fact that customers were using different systems, so suppliers like Hella had to learn to work with many different approaches, putting an increased load on already scarce skills and equipment.

The transition in design had two components — a people side and a system side.

On the people side there was a significant imbalance; most of the older designers had grown up with drawing boards and were unhappy or unwilling to make the change. At the time, around half of the designers were already over 50 years old and so there was a significant 'reprogramming' challenge to get them to accept the new technology. Recruiting new staff from universities and colleges was part of the solution but it was important to give them an understanding of the Hella context. Fortunately there were enough older experienced designers available to act as coaches to them.

On the hardware side the IBM systems was extremely expensive at a time when the company had a limited IT budget. That had the consequence that new workplaces could only be created in stepwise fashion as the money became available to acquire new workstations. For a while the design team worked on a shift basis to maximize this investment but that posed problems in big projects where the handover between shifts opened up error possibilities. Gradually the approach proved itself, not least in the speed and flexibility which it opened up.

There were also technical limits — some elements of the CAD system were not well suited to Hella's kind of electronics. IBM's machines were particularly well-matched for high complexity integrated circuit design layout but Hella was more concerned with linking mechanical and electronics design. Trying to get the system to work in new ways posed big problems, adding delays and errors and forcing a search for alternative solutions. Once again Hella was forced to adapt and develop its own way through the problem — in the process continuing to build its own highly specialized capability.

ASICS — application-specific integrated circuits — became increasingly important in the game. The first of these were used in blinkers (turn indicators) so Hella had already built up experience and the company approach was to design their own custom masks and circuits. It helped with the increasingly important area of intellectual property protection (IP) because it moved IP into hardware, which was much less easy to reverse engineer. During the highly competitive Lopez era this became an important advantage.

One problem with this hardware approach was that it locked the design 20 weeks or more ahead so changes weren't possible — reducing new product development freedom. But customers often wanted last-minute adjustments which were difficult to implement except via complex workarounds. Moving to a digital, software-based approach gave Hella the time needed and the flexibility to accommodate this.

Their approach was essentially to adopt a platform — pick a family of processors and then develop standard training, libraries of routines, standardized modules, etc., which gave flexibility and speed. (This was an early example of 'platform thinking', a theme to which we'll return in Chapter 9.)

Another important input was the early adoption of structured programming techniques. These were introduced originally using an external coach who spent a great deal of time training and supporting Hella's acquisition of such capability. After two years it became standard Hella practice and brought with it advantages of higher quality and faster development of software.

1985 also saw efforts towards total quality management of software — making sure errors were captured and not repeated. Through a mixture of protocols, checklists and standardized approaches the software development capability was strengthened and systematized.

But there was still a fundamental capacity problem — growth in demand meant that Hella couldn't get hold of enough engineers to carry the electronics wave forward. It resorted to using personal networks and made connection to ENKO, a small spin-off from the Olympia group which specialized in software. They began working in a contract basis for Hella (especially supplying test capacity) and eventually supplied 20–30 staff, supporting both the mainstream electronics development and also the growing future developments operation. Hella took over a majority stake in the business some years later and eventually it became a fully owned subsidiary, Hella Engineering, with around 60 specialist employees.

Another advantage for Hella in the early entry days was that (with the exception of VW) none of their major customers had their own in-house electronics capability. This allowed Hella to make its home-grown solutions into the industry standard whilst at the same time establishing a reputation as a preferred trusted supplier of quality electronics.

The next milestone on the journey lay not in the electronics themselves but in the connecting cables between them. As cars and the electronic systems became more complex and widespread so the problem of cabling rose to prominence. The solution lay in the idea of a BUS — using software to encode and decode different packets of information travelling along a single channel.

On the back of the strong reputation it had built as a competent technology partner Hella was increasingly invited by major customers to explore ideas together — for example, using a BUS approach for chassis electronics. Hella's system skills, covering both hardware and software, and its close links with semiconductor manufacturers and other key suppliers placed it in a strong position as a technologically competent partner.

From an early start in the 1980s Hella moved to a position of strength in electronics. By the mid-1990s over 1.8 million electronic modules per day were coming off Hella production lines. Some idea of the rapid progress can be gained from **Table 4.1** which shows a timeline for electronics innovation in Hella.

And in a major international benchmarking study carried out by McKinsey consultants working with the University of Darmstadt, Hella was ranked 14th out of 57 German electronics suppliers in terms of overall performance.

INNOVATION MODEL INNOVATION — 'DIE ÄNDERUNG'

From a technical point of view this progress was impressive — but from an innovation management point of view the accelerating

Table 4.1. Some Milestones in Hella's Electronics Innovation.

Year	Innovation
1965	First indicator flasher unit
1969	Wash wipe interval controller
1973	Seat belt warning
1976	Bulb monitoring system
1976	Electro-pneumatic speed regulator
1980	World's first dynamic oil level sensor
1982	Seat memory control
1984	First electronic climate control
1988	First ABS control for motorcycles
1989	First drive slip control for Audi 1989
1997	Integrated drive pedal sensor for drive by wire

pace of change had begun to create problems. The pattern which had built up over a decade for electronics at Hella was essentially similar to a start-up. Fast growth, a lot of luck, some unexpected benefits arising from having to find creative solutions to resource shortages — but essentially an entrepreneurial approach, ducking and diving, bobbing and weaving and somehow managing to grow. Very exciting, mostly successful, but at times lacking much in the way of system and structure.

As we saw in Chapter 2 a major review identified that only a small proportion of the projects accounted for most of the value being created. Of around 4,000 projects studied:

- 95 products were responsible for around 80% of turnover and 34% of R&D costs

- 305 were responsible for 15% turnover and 35% R&D

- 3,100 were responsible for 5% of turnover and 31% of R&D

This was the trigger for a major change programme — 'die Änderung' (the change) — involving a complete overhaul aimed at bringing in a portfolio approach linked to a clear market strategy, developing closer functional integration and streamlining product development processes. Prior to this there were small 'empires', each working independently and only loosely connected — for example there were no less than nine Deputy Managing Directors responsible for various areas.

Before 'Die Änderung' (the change) took place these had oper-ated as very different worlds. As one interviewee explained, *'It used to be that manufacturing did what they were told, never got or gave feedback. Equally no designer knew the price of his changes — there was no cost consciousness. Neither component cost nor final selling price ... And R&D never went near Production — that was forbidden!'*

Inevitably this meant inefficient use of resources and real risks of duplication of effort. The 'change' brought the different worlds closer together — for example, measurement test equipment developed and implemented in parallel with the production people. The 1996 recommendations included establishing clear portfolio management to aid selection and resource allocation to development projects and the adoption of a product management approach. Seven Product Managers were appointed supported by customer-facing Key Account Managers reporting to them for all the key product groups.

After 18 months it was already clear that the new system was making a difference, a view expressed by Karl-Heinz Krücken in an interview with the company newspaper in January 1998. Through adopting the Product Management (PM) approach the team were able to focus on promising product lines and the concept of internal factories helped concentrate all necessary resources and knowledge towards their delivery. A good example of concrete differences between the old and new system was in the role played by the 'master plan' in targeting resources; under the old system different elements (lighting components or electronic components) of new products were produced in different places whereas, with the new system, they are all brought together in the same place. Another big difference is the relationship with customers which now benefits from the key account management (KAM) approach. Decision-making is much simpler now, running through PM and KAM rather than dispersed through various levels and functions.

It was not an overnight shift — what was effectively a full scale innovation model took three years for the separate functional areas to gradually integrate into a modern stage gate process with portfolio management, product managers and project management discipline. Importantly, this change — and the preceding years of successful growth and accumulation of competence — was steered by internal champions like Waldeyer, Krucken and Trowitsch. While McKinsey provided some helpful ideas and templates, and senior management gave overall support, much of the culture change that established GE (Geschäftsbereich Elektronik) as the strong platform on which the next 20 years of company growth were based comes down to their efforts and those of other internal entrepreneurs.

Climate Control

Sit in any new car today — and you expect climate control. Whether it is to keep you warm in the depths of an Eastern European winter or to cool you as you speed along summer motorways in the south of France, climate control has become a standard feature which people expect. And enabling it is about much more than wrapping rugs around your legs or keeping the windows wide open — it's a complex arrangement of sensors, actuators and mechanical components.

But it wasn't always so — and the process of bringing this technology first into luxury vehicles and then developing it in terms of cost and engineering to become available to the mass market is something Hella has pioneered.

The first thinking about climate control (as opposed to a simple heater) inside a car began in 1979–1980 and involved a water valve for the water side of the heater system. A major customer had been working with the French company, Sofica Thermal (part of the Valeo group), and suggested they collaborate with Hella in an arrangement where Sofica would work on the thermal part and Hella the electronics. They could test it in Sofica's climate and wind tunnel facility.

This worked well and led Hella to develop their own concept for a water-based heater control which would be tested with a major customer in 1982. Between 1984 and 1986 extensive work went on with a different customer producing high performance luxury cars, effectively 'pushing the envelope' in terms of what climate control might offer.

Characteristic of the approach taken was the 'probe and learn' prototyping now common in discussions of 'agile innovation' and 'lean start-up'. Friedrich Waldeyer and Karl-Heinz Krücken experimented with various approaches, working to get not only the technical functions working but also thinking about issues like acoustics and comfort — the 'look, feel and touch' side of the story as they put it. The lack of test facilities meant they did a great deal of learning by doing, experimenting on themselves and weaving together an understanding of both the physiology and the psychology of comfort in the car. It also gave them a user perspective, seeing the role of things like weather conditions from that standpoint rather than from that of car technologists. This helped them build a deep understanding that they were able to translate into hardware and software.

The combination of their electronic and mechanical engineering skills helped in this prototyping — but so too did an entrepreneurial style of working. Having heard that the Chairman of one of their major luxury car customers was keen on having climate control they worked on a prototype, fitted it into a production car and then drove it over to him to offer a first-hand taste of the experience. This was a high-risk strategy but in the event he was impressed and this support gave strong impetus to subsequent development work. Their team grew from the two of them at the outset to 30 people.

In 1987 a redesign brought a significant cost reduction and quality improvement. The positive response from the market for early models led Hella to develop a new system for this in 1989 which used a combination of a butterfly valve on the exhaust heat exchanger and then an airside controlled air conditioner, all handled by a specially developed controller. With this they were able to move from low volume luxury car applications into the high volume market.

At around the same time VW in Wolfsburg began developing a new heating system and introduced it in 1989–1991. As part of the drive by VW's Purchasing Director Ignacio Lopez to push down prices a broader application of climate and heating control systems was promoted — spreading the cost but increasing the application over a wider range of vehicles. Through a series of intensive workshops Hella explored all possible ways of reducing costs — value engineering; for example, major emphasis was placed on using ASICs to cut the number of components and improve their quality/reliability. This made it possible to reduce, for example, the cost of climate control for some models by over 50%.

The result of all of this was that Hella could offer the option of climate control and inner cabin comfort at a competitive price — opening up the potential mass market. As their position strengthened in this field it made sense for Hella to establish a dedicated business, teaming up in 1999 with Behr, another specialist, to create BHTC — Behr-Hella Thermocontrol — which has become a key business in the wider Hella group.

From the early days of experimenting through to this very profitable business had taken 20 years — but it was by no means a simple 'plug and play' product development. Instead it drew on several strategic elements, not least their deep competence in electronics, which mean they had the core expertise around sensors and actuators and, later, around ASICs, which helped them reduce cost and modularize the concept. They were also experienced in bridging between the electronic and mechanical world, specializing in systems rather than components.

This competence was also recognized in a marketplace in which Hella had proved itself a reliable and capable partner and one with whom it was safe to experiment with new ideas. An indication of the preferred status which this gave was that Hella had a full team-working in Munich at the BMW plant alongside their engineers.

The strategy of working with demanding needs of the luxury car market also meant that Hella was in a strong position to capture the lessons and engineer applications for a much wider downstream market. At the same time the VW/Lopez experience had forced them to consider radical cost saving approaches early on; the result was that Hella had '*both the best products and the best prices!*'.

Xenon — Another Example of Pioneering

Climate control is only one example of a product area which has benefitted from both a commitment to deep technological competence and also entrepreneurial champions to help channel that knowledge into a series of innovations. Similar patterns can be found in the core lighting side where Hella has led the field in headlamp technology for decades. The case of Xenon lights is a good example.

In 1988 Hella joined a European Union research project under the EUREKA programme to work with partners to develop a new kind of headlight system based on a pressurized gas discharge lamp which offered an extremely short arc. It would have a long lifetime, high performance and be suited to vehicle application. The 'VEDILIS' project was a four-year programme with key partners from across Europe with interests in lighting — GE Lighting (UK), Carello (Italy) Philips (Netherlands), Valeo (France) and Osram, Bosch and Hella from Germany.

The project had three phases — defining the research area and developing prototypes, exploring and field testing in application areas and finally scaling up and standardizing. Philips was the key partner in Eindhoven; they already had a prototype of a lamp so there was a solid technology base on which to build. Bosch and Hella decided early on that this had potential for car lighting and agreed to an exchange of ideas and experiences in order to progress the concept.

Internally this project provided an opportunity for closer working between the light technology and the electronics area in Hella. Since the discharge lamp technology required fast control of a high-speed load and discharge cycle the question was raised as to whether they would buy in the electronic part (e.g. from Bosch) or design their own. The decision was taken to develop their own, helped by the lucky availability of a discharge lamp expert from Frankfurt who was prepared to work on a contract basis. He had extensive experience in film studio arc lamp design and worked alongside two Hella engineers who had experience in the field of high voltage electronics in colour television. So they had the nucleus of a small team which was later expanded with two designers. But this was a small team compared with the efforts at Bosch who had over 20 people devoted to the project.

In the early days of developing prototypes a number of technical problems had to be overcome, not least the fact that the operating principle meant that very high voltages had to be switched on and off very fast (within milliseconds) and with high precision. This constant switching on and off put considerable wear on the electrodes so that the life of the bulb was another problem and it was hard to reach the proposed target of 3,000 hours. In order to solve the problem they needed a test facility that would allow them to experiment with changing different parameters and run the lamps for long enough to prove their reliability.

Hella decided to install their own test facility and located this right next to the project team, enabling the learning process around building understanding of how to control such new lamp technology.

On the customer side a major manufacturer decided at a very early stage to put Xenon lamps in their vehicles and had three test versions of one of their models fitted with prototypes, one in the electronics group and two in the headlight group. These were given permits to drive as prototypes on the open road.

Unfortunately (or perhaps not in terms of the subsequent future of the innovation) the winter of 1989–1990 was particularly cold in north Germany with continuous snow. It quickly became clear that under cold conditions the lamps weren't able to cope. In particular their low operating temperature meant that snow wouldn't melt on the glass and so they were modified to use windscreen washers on the headlamps as was obligatory in Scandinavia.

Another problem which emerged from the road testing was headlight levelling. This had to be very fast due to the sensitive nature of the lamps whose beam was affected by even small potholes and surface problems and 'normal' automatic levelling systems didn't work. Worse, on rough stretches of road the lamps themselves would switch off because the arc could not be maintained, and then there was a dark delay while they were restarted!

None of these were insurmountable problems but the early prototyping — what would in today's jargon be called using a 'minimum viable product' — meant that the teams could focus on the key issues quickly. They drew on broad expertise from across the collaborating network — for example, around the resonance ignition system which Hella had decided to use. Extensive testing showed that after 50 hours of operation problems arose leading to lamp fade out; Philips' experience suggested that this was a problem with the switching circuit wearing out the electrodes and eventually an alternative switching approach was used. The free flow of knowledge at this pre-competitive stage was a key feature of the project — and an early example of 'open innovation'.

Like any development project solving one problem moved the focus elsewhere and in this case the different switching system posed problems in manufacturing. The particular key operation involved casting under vacuum and was sub-contracted out to a specialist manufacturer who had extensive experience of something similar in the colour television industry. Once again an example of open innovation — key knowledge flowing in from outside.

A key breakthrough came in 1990 when the Japanese firm TDK began offering a switch which could be easily incorporated and solved the lifetime problem for the lamps. Hella procured a number of these for evaluation and tests showed they did work — but this raised the question of whether to buy-in such a key component or to develop their own version. Under some pressure the

Hella team worked hard to come up with their own version within a short three-month period and eventually succeeded. So the control unit could be contained within an integrated circuit assembly — a significant breakthrough but again one which challenged the production side who had to incorporate another set of new technologies in their process.

The story illustrates several key elements — for example, the early collaborative approach to creating knowledge ('open innovation') but also the recognition of where and when it is important to invest in the (risky) business of creating and owning key knowledge (as in the TDK replacement). It is about fast learning with customers and rapid prototyping to highlight and focus on key areas — and the need to pivot development work in the light of lessons learned. 'Fast failure' is another phrase often associated with start-ups but, as this case shows, being able to work with this model and to respond and redirect effort provides a powerful accelerator to innovation. The happy ending of the story is that Hella was the first to introduce Xenon lamps on a production basis and this has given them a strong market position.

The experience of Xenon lamps was not an exception; Hella's systematic approach to developing deep understanding around lighting technology allied to a willingness to experiment and prototype early led them to pioneer the application of light-emitting diode (LED) systems in the following years. Initial exploration began in the 1970s and by 1982 Hella had become the first European manufacturer to supply an LED brake light system as a standard feature on a customer's volume production model. The range of applications soon spread from brake lights to indicators and eventually to headlights themselves.

Rethinking the Hella Production System

The automobile industry has a long history of process innovation, dating back, of course, to Henry Ford and his team of engineers pioneering the principles of mass production. And once established this became a dominant model, not only for making cars but also for the volume manufacture of pretty much anything.

However, in the 1980s, the industry underwent something of a revolution in thinking, driven by a powerful research study called 'the future of the automobile'. This was conceived as a major review of innovation in the industry, looking at both product and process changes and best practices and was funded by all the major car manufacturers. An important feature of this research was the role played by the university consortium (led by MIT) which allowed each manufacturer to share openly what they were thinking and doing, secure in the knowledge that they would all benefit from the aggregated and anonymized picture of the industry and how they stacked up against this.

The product innovation story was interesting, showing patterns of leadership in the USA with the wave of early product variety, followed by concentration and standardization around Ford's Model T and subsequent differentiation by designing models to serve different segments. This was followed by a shift to product differentiation with European manufacturers contributing a variety of designs linked to specific regional requirements.

But the real shock was in the process innovation data that emerged following a systematic study of productivity in 68 assembly plants around the world. These revealed big differences:

> *... our findings were eye-opening. The Japanese plants*
> *require one-half the effort of the American luxury-car*
> *plants, half the effort of the best European plant, a quarter*
> *of the effort of the average European plant, and one-sixth*
> *the effort of the worst European luxury car producer. At*
> *the same time, the Japanese plant greatly exceeds the qual-*
> *ity level of all plants except one in Europe — and this*
> *European plant required four times the effort of the*
> *Japanese plant to assemble a comparable product ....*[3]

Needless to say it drove non-Japanese manufacturers to a frenzy of exploration trying to find out which approaches were being used and how to adopt them quickly. Various hypotheses were explored around automation but despite considerable investment in this direction it gradually emerged that the real secret lay in the alternative approach the Japanese car industry had been forced to take during the decades after the Second World War. Resource shortages, a small domestic market and lack of skilled labour meant that they needed to evolve a low waste approach, one which emphasized the underlying organization and management of production. The university researchers christened this philosophy 'lean manufacturing' and the name stuck; it involved a mixture of techniques including employee involvement in sustained incremental innovation ('kaizen'), 'just-in-time' production based on a pull rather than push philosophy and particularly the idea of eliminating all non-value adding activities and enabling smooth flow along the value stream.

By the 1990s severe pressure was being put on all carmakers to match Japanese productivity levels and in addition to their own efforts at getting lean they began to pass on the message to their suppliers, calling for significant improvements in cost, quality and delivery performance.

Spearheading this was Ignacio Lopez, at the time Purchasing Director for GM and later VW. For him this became a personal crusade pursued with almost religious fervour — one of many quotations from him reveals the passion with which he embraced the need for lean: '... *The world is at war ... the battle for the automobile industry is the final struggle ... if we lose it, we shall become second-class citizens in second-class countries!*'.

His approach while working as head of GM purchasing in Europe involved radical challenges, ripping up long-standing contracts, ending cosy relationships and demanding ever-lower prices, steadily improving quality and sparking faster deliveries. Simultaneously he was developing his Plateau 8 lean-manufacturing principles and pushing suppliers to adopt them. His approach saved GM Europe millions, making Opel's supplier costs the lowest in Europe. In 1991 he was summoned to Detroit where he worked the same approach on the US parent's network, cutting $1.1 billion from the purchasing bill by 1992 with planned savings for 1993 as high as $2.4 billion.

He then left GM to join Volkswagen, arguing that the same cuts coupled with productivity gains of around 30% on the part of suppliers could be achieved.

His core philosophy was that prices were no longer to be set by production costs. Rather, production costs had to be tailored to the prices that clients would accept. Having established such a price, he would then take a margin for the supplier — 'since obviously they must make a profit' — and whatever is left is production costs plus the car company's own profit. This usually implied a drop of 20–30%.

Again, a quotation illustrates his tough stance: '... *I do not want to hear any more that prices are already down too far and you are making no profits .... We have to change our attitudes. No more excuses. Instead, creativity in action, in a process of continuous improvement*'. But it was not simply a matter of getting tough with suppliers; he also offered to help them improve by adopting lean principles. He had assembled teams to do this while working at Opel and these now moved across VW's supplier base. The idea behind these 'Picos' (Purchased Input Concept Optimization with Suppliers) teams developed over time but their influence was significant. In a study of 40 suppliers with whom they worked, average improvements included productivity, lead time, inventory holding and production area needed as represented (Table 4.2).

For Hella this posed particular problems. First they found themselves suddenly in the firing line when Lopez moved to Volkswagen since VW were such a significant partner for Hella. And second, Hella's relatively small size meant it was difficult to

Table 4.2. Key Performance Improvements Across the Industry Achieved Through New Approaches.

Productivity	+42%
Lead time	−49%
Inventory holding	−57%
Production area needed	−30%

Table 4.3. Performance Improvements in Hella Production Activities.

Labour input required	−27%
Assembly time	−30%
Work-in-progress inventory	−99%
Space required	−82%
Throughput time	−99%

find cost reductions through scale economies or by spreading to other plants in locations with cheaper costs. So there was an urgent need to change — and change fast. As Jürgen Behrend put it, it was a simple question — to be or not to be!

Their first move was to benchmark themselves against not only other suppliers of automotive components but much wider electronics. The level of detail is instructive — this was a full-scale deep dive to understand best practice and the specific gaps to delivering it. This forced a major rethink about their approach to assembly and machinery. They sourced expertise from Japan and began the journey of change which spread first through all their German factories and then to their foreign plants.

In April 1991 they held a series of discussions which set targets for rethinking their approach, and throughout the following year they held a series of management seminars and shop-floor workshops, and explored some pilot applications of lean.

Pilot projects such as one in the area of climate control equipment showed that it was possible to achieve significant savings (Table 4.3).

By the end of 1992 they had developed their own version of lean linked to a kaizen approach, and by 1995 they had absorbed and integrated key principles into what became the Hella Production System (HPS), emulating the powerful Toyota Production System model. HPS was a philosophy supported by core principles:

- Zero defects
- Efficient product launch
- Controlled supply chain
- Continuous improvement and standardization
- Supporting and challenging employees

It was enabled by using a suite of over 30 proven methods and 50 tools (such as 5S, kanban, value engineering, poke yoke and value stream analysis). Responsibility for implementing HPS in these areas was overseen by a Steering Group and implementation was led by strategy teams in five key areas.

The overall model was similar to most lean approaches around at the time — its power lay in it being a home developed and configured version. This was a Hella Production System, not a 'plug and play' import from outside. Its success lay in its widespread adoption and support from a workforce challenged by the external crisis but also motivated by support from within. The principle of 'entrepreneurial responsibility' played an important role and one indicator of its success was the dramatic increase in employee suggestions from around 1,300 in 1993 to 13,000 by 1997.

The model was further refined in 2006 and in 2010 where they used it to drive towards a 2ppm Top Company status. Developing and implementing HPS enabled the company not only to survive the difficult Lopez years but also to emerge as a competitive manufacturer working at world class levels of lean performance.

By 1997 the changes (not just HPS but also efforts around standardization, developing a flexible automation approach based on modular systems rolled out worldwide, revising the make/buy strategy and other innovations) had worked and Hella moved out of crisis and back into profitability.

Once again the underlying pattern can be seen. Major strategic direction from the top — in this case a powerful external threat — and careful use of expert advice from outside followed through by internal entrepreneurs, change agents like Karl-Heinz Krücken and Thomas Netterscheid. The latter had joined the company back in the late 1960s and had been a part of a small but dedicated team working on process innovation since then. Much of the success in rethinking of production was enabled by the strong team spirit which came from that group. Their efforts were particularly based around learning by doing, by improvising Hella's own versions of proven solutions and finding their own routes (e.g. with specialist automation) to solve problems.

Creating the Innovation Engine for the Future

Organizations need to innovate to survive, of course. Unless they change their offerings (products/services) and the ways in which they create and deliver those (process innovation) they may not be around in the long term. History is clear on that matter and companies like Hella are well aware of the innovation imperative. But it takes more than the strategic will to innovate — the organization needs to do something to make innovation happen. As we've seen this involves building both knowledge competence and also the innovation management capability to turn that knowledge into value.

Hella's commitment to R&D has been consistent and strong for decades but it still needs to confront the challenge of where to invest that resource. One helpful way of looking at this is to think in terms of three 'horizons' — if R&D is about looking forward then it might help to separate out frames in which to explore the future (**Figure** 4.2).[4]

The first horizon — typically extending from today forward to 18 months — is very much about the supporting R&D needed to ensure the edge which products and services have can be preserved. It is focused incremental innovation together with progression of some core strategic projects, which will come to fruition during that time period. In many ways it is a 'harvesting' investment — the crops have been sown and nurtured and the investment here is to ensure good yields as they are gathered in.

The second horizon (typically 12–36 months) looks further out; to stay with the agricultural metaphor these are the green shoots of potential new business. These need to be sown and carefully tended; the challenge here is to target R&D into those areas which show promise and have growth potential when they mature.

And the third horizon (typically 24–72 months) is all about creating new opportunities in the future. It's about watching technological and market trends and trying to spot those of potential

Figure 4.2. Three Horizons in Innovation Thinking.

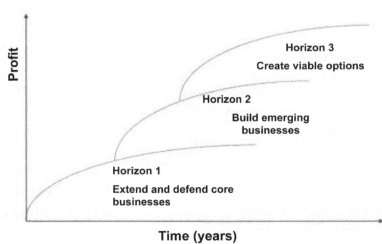

importance and then making careful investments to monitor and
beginning to lay the groundwork — preparing the soil in our
farming analogy.

Of course these are simplistic frames but they do suggest that
R&D strategy needs to strike a balance between these and to find
ways of ensuring that what comes out of one horizon feeds well
into the next. The company needs a long-term roadmap for the
highway it is driving down.

Hella began to create capacity for horizon 3 thinking back
in 1967 when they established a small 'future developments'
(Zukunftsentwicklung (ZE)) team. One of its original members was
Eberhard Zuckmantel who remained with the group through its
various incarnations until he retired in 2001. ZE was originally seen
as a separate team, a staff function rather than aligned with mainstream product development (essentially horizon 1 and 2 activity).

An advertisement was placed in the Frankfurter Allgemeine
Zeitung in October 1966 calling for engineers to play three roles —
team leader, designer and calculations engineer — working towards
the goal of expanding the horizons for the business. (Interestingly,
the company name was deliberately excluded.) The team was
formed, comprising Zuckmantel, Karl-Heinz Krücken and another
colleague, and they began working on 1 January 1967.

In the early stages their numbers fluctuated between three and
five staff and they worked on a mixture of projects based around
electronics and plastics. In 1974 the plastics work was moved into
the mainstream development area and ZE concentrated exclu-
sively on electronics and electrical development. They provided
valuable support and direction to the growing electronics capability, especially during the early 1980s when the company was
moving into new technological territory.

With the major re-organization of product development in electronics in the 1990s came a rethink of the role of ZE and it was
expanded and positioned more clearly as a futures group, working
to horizon 2 and 3. The group grew (through redeployment of

existing development staff rather than new recruitment) to 15 strong.

ACCELERATING INNOVATION IN ELECTRONICS

By the early 2000s electronics had become a main powerhouse alongside the Lighting division, one driven by increasing R&D investment to drive through new focused products. Part of the McKinsey legacy was a much stronger market orientation and this had led to significant growth in the Advanced Engineering area responsible for new product development. A new manager, Michael Jaeger, joined Hella as a member of the Executive Board of GE in 2012, coming from Bosch where he had spent time in new product development. His role included leading the development of innovation management capability across the division.

He undertook a review of activities and, based on Board level discussion, there was an appetite to explore the balance between horizon 1 activity (which consumed the majority of the significant R&D spend) and more long-term exploration. Working with external consultants, proposals were made for a new AE structure which would rebalance activities, providing not only a clear focus for horizon 1 work but also pathways and processes for wider and longer-term exploration. Learning the lessons from the 1990s around unfocused exploration this approach placed considerable emphasis on end-user applications (use cases) and the convergence of technological trends with these emerging demand possibilities.

Workshops looking at both technology and market trends helped identify several key strategic areas in which Hella could and should play — for example, in advanced car security, electro mobility and green technology. These were termed Hella Focus Areas (HFAs), representing strategic priorities within which horizon 2 and 3 exploration could take place. By 2014 several of these had been systematically explored and four in particular were singled out:

- Car access

- Road condition detection and lane keeping

- Vehicle energy management

- Reducing energy consumption

A series of 'lighthouse projects' were defined in these areas where there was good fit between Hella competence and knowledge base and end user needs.

Teams were allocated to spend some time on these projects in parallel with mainstream horizon 1 activities.

Central to this was the idea not of random exploration of future trends but of identifying clear roadmaps to guide development work. In terms of an innovation process this future mapping added a 'scouting' opportunity search to front-end processes through which further ideation, development and implementation could take place.

Several other strands were linked in this rethink of AE, including exploring ways of tapping internal entrepreneurship in a more open fashion through some form of innovation contest. With the support of a specialist consultancy who provided the collaboration platform (Venture Spirit) Hella launched 'Driving e-novation'.

This coupled additional ideation capability — and broadcast search rather than functional search — around some of the key HFAs. Initial project ideas were sought in:

- Autonomous driving and safety

- Ease of use

- Car to x communication

- Increased car efficiency

As the initial announcement indicated:

Driving e-novation is an online business competition within the Hella Electronics Division that stimulates the innovation culture and entrepreneurship through global and cross-functional collaboration while looking for new innovative opportunities

There is a more extensive discussion of this in Chapter 6.

2015 saw further exploring of the challenges of dealing with an increasingly uncertain future and led to the establishment of a new Hella operation, Hella Ventures with the remit of exploring potentially disruptive innovation and opportunities for Hella within that space. (Once again this theme is discussed in more detail in Chapter 11.)

These activities can be seen to be directly descended from the original decision some 50 years earlier to commit resource and capacity to exploring the future.

FURTHER RESOURCES

You can find a number of useful resources — case studies, video and audio, and tools to explore some of the themes discussed in this chapter at www.innovation-portal.info

In particular:

- Case study of the skunk works approach

- Case studies of organizations using online collaboration platforms to boost innovation — Liberty Global, Lufthansa Systems

- Tools and activities linked to core themes raised in the chapter

REFLECTION QUESTIONS

1. Choose an organization with which you are familiar and try to identify some internal innovators — champions of change.

What innovations did they help enable and what challenges did they face along the way?

2. Think about an internal innovation — an entrepreneur enabling change to happen. What challenges might they encounter in trying to promote change inside a large organization, and what strategies might they need to overcome these?

3. Drawing on examples of internal entrepreneurs making change happen what advice might you give to someone who has been given the opportunity to act as a change champion within a large organization?

NOTES

1. You can find a more extensive discussion around entrepreneurship, both internal and external, in John Bessant and Joe Tidd (2015).

2. See Rich and Janos (1994).

3. You can find more about the research underpinning lean thinking in Womack, Jones, and Roos (1991).

4. You can find more about the three horizons model, originally developed by McKinsey Consultants, in Bahghai, Coley, and White (1999).

5

MAINTAINING MOMENTUM

Managing innovation is all about keeping the pulse of change pumping in the bloodstream of any company. When Sally Windmüller first saw the opportunities opening up in the new automotive business he was acting as a classic entrepreneur. Finding resources, building networks, experimenting (sometimes failing) and gradually creating a business out of ideas. And so Hella was born.

But being a start-up isn't the best model for growing a business. Meeting the needs of a growing range of customers needs emphasis on process innovation — building a reliable factory to keep delivering the products. And with growing markets and new customers comes the requirement for a more systematic approach to new product development. Keeping up with fast-changing technology needs investment in creating new knowledge and connection to places (like universities and technical centres) where it can be found. And so the company grew through diversifying its approach to innovation, adding to its capabilities.

Any organization needs dynamic capability — the ability to update and extend the ways in which it meets the innovation challenge. As it grows and works in a more complex world so it needs to develop new capabilities to innovate in many directions and to strike a balance between 'doing what we do better' (incremental innovation) and 'doing something completely different' (radical innovation).

That's been the story of Hella — growing a successful business through innovation and riding the waves of change. Working with product innovation, exploiting increasingly sophisticated technology and building capabilities around key component areas. At the same time building its strengths in process innovation through commitment to quality, to operational excellence via lean principles, to logistics and moving to internet-enabled platforms. Becoming increasingly active in diverse markets — position innovation — through getting close to different customer groups in developed and emerging markets and locating facilities in those countries to provide valuable insights into local needs and conditions. And business model innovation — rethinking and extending what Hella is, beginning to explore new industries in which its competencies might be offered and rethinking its role as it starts to explore disruptive opportunities.

Underpinning this *'innovation model innovation'* is a core strategic value — 'entrepreneurial responsibility'. This is the glue which holds the different innovation models together and it is a mixture of top-down direction and commitment to innovation and bottom-up ideas, energy and enthusiasm driving for change.

Viewed from outside Hella has an impressive history with many milestone innovations in its products and processes and a continuing stream of new developments. That's come from a consistent commitment to innovation and to finding new ways to drive the process forward (**Figure 5.1**).

SO FAR, SO GOOD ...

The trouble with innovation is that it is a moving target. Things change — markets shift, technologies advance, competition emerges. So unless an organization is constantly adapting and

Figure 5.1. Key Components of Innovation-led Growth.

extending its routines it risks running out of steam — even if it has a strong history of innovation. Think of Kodak — one of the 'poster children' of the 20th Century, a growth from George Eastman's start-up to the world's biggest film company. Yet now it languishes, a shadow of its former self and struggling to develop a new identity in fields like printing. This wasn't a case of a foolish business missing out on an important new technology wave — it was the earliest entrant into the new world of digital media. The world's first patents, the first digital camera — all products of the knowledge powerhouse which was Kodak's R&D system. The problem came with its innovation routines — how it translated those deep knowledge competencies into value. Partly saddled with an established business model to which it was heavily committed, partly through an inability to be able to grow in new areas while letting go of its birth-right.[1]

Or IBM, another global business built on deep technological competencies matched by a rich market knowledge base. Once again the problem was not in what it knew but in how it translated that knowledge into value — its routines, capability. Faced with the growing trends towards decentralized computing and networks the company stubbornly retained its commitment to the mainframe centralized model and innovated along that trajectory —in the process nearly running the business over a cliff. It took a fresh perspective and a lot of wrestling to turn the wheel and begin the transformation towards the highly successful service and solutions business which IBM represents today.[2]

At the heart of this is the question of 'dynamic capability' — the second order capability, which allows an organization to review, adapt and refresh its innovation routines.[3] The ways in which it made innovation happen in the past may still be relevant, they may need adapting — and sometimes there is the need to create completely new routines. Building capabilities is a slow process — a mixture of trial and error, reinforcement and refining. And they are hard to let go of. Many analysts view Polaroid's decline as being more about an inability to change its routines for innovating to take advantage of the new digital media as being the cause of their problem rather than a lack of technological expertise.[4]

So a big question in staying on the innovation wave, riding it rather than being thrashed around by it, is how to keeping its innovation capabilities fresh and relevant. That's the challenge facing Hella today — a large company with a global presence and strong networks of connections with key customers and suppliers.

HOW WELL DOES HELLA MANAGE INNOVATION?

How well does Hella manage innovation? One answer has to be 'well enough' since the company has survived and grown over its 100 plus year history. It has a long expressed belief in innovation and backs this up with investments which have consistently been close to 10% of turnover reinvested in R&D. Around a fifth of its increasingly global workforce is involved in developing new products, processes and services and it is extensively networked into key strategic technology areas.

But these are all input measures — evidence of a commitment to innovation and a willingness to invest strategically in the area. The real question is around innovation management capability — how well are they able to build a knowledge base and successfully translate it into value?

Innovation research tells us that this capability is not a single thing but a cluster of behaviours embedded deep in the processes and policies of the organization. It includes the ways in which they tackle challenges of searching for opportunities, selecting, implementing and capturing value, and it brings in issues like strategic direction and developing a supportive innovation culture.

Figure 5.2 offers a simple model which highlights these question areas.[5]

It is worth starting with these core questions and looking at how well Hella handles them. **Table** 5.1 provides a short summary; the left hand column indicating the kind of response we might expect from an organization managing these things well.

Figure 5.2. Simple Model of Innovation Management Capability.

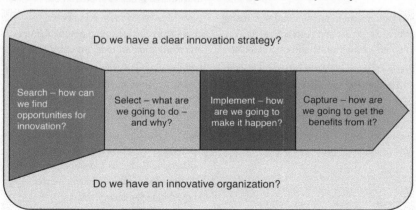

Table 5.1. How Well Does Hella Manage Innovation?

Key Area	How Well Does Hella Perform?
(a) Searching for opportunities	
We have good relationships with our suppliers and we pick up a steady stream of ideas from them	Close links built up with key technology suppliers like semiconductor companies.
We are good at understanding the needs of our customers/end-users	Since the 1996 reorganization the model of product management has meant that these links are close with major car manufacturers. Increasingly, emphasis is placed, at early stage product development planning, on the idea of carefully constructed use cases, bringing in this understanding.
We work well with universities and other research centres to help us develop our knowledge	Close links with key players in Germany, perhaps less well-developed on a wider basis.
Our people are involved in suggesting ideas for improvements to products or processes	The principle of entrepreneurial responsibility means that ideas are actively sought. There are several channels in addition to formal product and process development — for example, the continuous improvement programmes that have been running in different forms since the 1990s or the increasing use of idea contests in product development, and now moving into process improvement.
We look ahead in a structured way (using forecasting tools and techniques) to imagine future threats and opportunities	Since the 1960s there has been a commitment to exploring potential futures, and tools and methods are deployed.
We systematically compare our products and processes with other firms	Hella makes use of benchmarks and other forms of research, and has done for some time — for example, the 1990s McKinsey Darmstadt University study.
We collaborate with other firms to develop new products or processes	Much of Hella's success goes back to the 1990s and the ideas behind strategic networking — building collaborations and alliances to be able to deliver increasingly knowledge-intensive products.

Table 5.1. (*Continued*)

Key Area	How Well Does Hella Perform?
We try to develop external networks of people who can help us — for example, with specialist knowledge	Multiple examples of external networking and engagement of specialist consultants and advisors.
We work closely with 'lead users' to develop innovative new products and services	A key theme in recent strategy has been to work with the demanding customers like those making luxury and high performance cars. Meeting their needs creates an envelope and enables downstream spread of these products into mass market segments and higher volume production.

(b) Selecting innovation projects

We have a clear system for choosing innovation projects and everyone understands the rules of the game in making proposals	There is a clear and systematic process, originally introduced during the 1996 reorganization and now well-established as a way of filling a portfolio and controlling progress through stage gates.
When someone has a good idea they know how to take it forward	There are a growing number of routes to enable employee ideas to move forward — for example, via the innovation contests.
We have a selection system which tries to build a balanced portfolio of low and high risk projects	Again, since 1996 there has been a clear product/market strategy and the use of portfolio techniques to enable its execution.
We focus on a mixture of product, process, market and business model innovation	Hella's history has been primarily about product innovation and the process changes, which enable the development and production of those. But there has also been considerable position innovation — first through internationalization and expansion into adjacent markets and, more recently, into positioning Hella as a strategic technology partner, changing the dominant narrative.
We balance projects for 'do better' innovation with some efforts on the radical, 'do different' side	Since the 1996 reorganization there have been attempts to ensure a balance between innovation horizons, allowing for some proportion of effort to be spent on 'do different' projects. More recent developments in this direction have included the setting up of Hella Ventures to provide structures and frameworks for systematic exploration at the edges of Hella's current world.

Table 5.1. *(Continued)*

Key Area	How Well Does Hella Perform?
We recognize the need to work 'outside the box' and there are mechanisms for handling 'off message' but interesting ideas	This has been an area of increasing concern and a number of initiatives have been explored — including open idea contests and Hella Ventures.
We have structures for corporate venturing	Informally, these are in place but one area in which Hella has now started to move has been in establishing a new group — Hella Ventures — to play this role. See Chapters 10 and 11 for more details.

(c) Implementing innovation

We have clear and well-understood formal processes in place to help us manage new product development effectively from idea to launch	Established in the 1990s and now providing a powerful framework for control; the main concern is that the structure of such processes may inhibit certain kinds of innovation which is why the recent moves to find parallel approaches have been made.
Our innovation projects are usually completed on time and within budget	Increasingly true and the basis for Hella's growing success in the marketplace.
We have effective mechanisms for managing process change from idea through to successful implementation	From its early years Hella has built parallel process capability to support the development and introduction of new products, and maintains a strong tradition of process innovation. Examples of this strategic capability include the development of the Hella Production System, the automation strategy and current exploration of advanced and intelligent automation around concepts of 'Industry 4.0'.
We have mechanisms in place to ensure early involvement of all departments in developing new products/processes	Since the early 1990s (where there was a major initiative to re-organize product development) considerable attention has been paid to ensuring close involvement between functional areas and early involvement across disciplines. Work on platform projects has further enhanced this close collaborative model.

Table 5.1. *(Continued)*

Key Area	How Well Does Hella Perform?
There is sufficient flexibility in our system for product development to allow small 'fast track' projects to happen	Recognition of the challenges has led to focused exploration around 'agile' innovation and where and when such approaches would help.
Our project teams for taking innovation forward involve people from all the relevant parts of the organization	Increasing cross-functional involvement, particularly around platform projects. Owes much to earlier reorganization in the 1990s setting the pattern for such co-operation.
We involve everyone with relevant knowledge from the beginning of the process	This approach follows lessons learned during the 1990s and now extends to increasing levels of 'open innovation' across the company.

(d) Innovation strategy

People in this organization have a clear idea of how innovation can help us compete	Internal communications replay the strong external message of Hella as a technological leader with innovation at the heart of its DNA.
There is a clear link between the innovation projects we carry out and the overall strategy of the business	Regular communication helps focus on this theme and link the high investment in R&D to clear business objectives.
We have processes in place to review new technological or market developments and what they mean for our firm's strategy	Formally reviewed on a regular basis as part of annual strategic reviews and also discussed at i-Circle as a wider community of practice.
There is top management commitment and support for innovation	Long-running strength of the company and clear from the fact that many key initiatives have top-level sponsorship.
Our top team have a shared vision of how the company will develop through innovation	There is clear consistency and regular discussion of innovation at Board level and via the i-Circle.
We look ahead in a structured way (using forecasting tools and techniques) to imagine future threats and opportunities	Hella has had a future scanning operation since the 1960s and has developed extensive capability using internal and external sources to create use cases and future trend information to guide innovation.
People in the organization know what our distinctive competence is — what gives us a competitive edge	There is good recognition of the deep competencies around lighting — exemplified in products and in key

Table 5.1. (*Continued*)

Key Area	How Well Does Hella Perform?
	equipment such as the Lichtkanal — and in electronics where increasingly it is Hella's position as a supplier of intelligent sensors and actuators that is driving the market position.
Our innovation strategy is clearly communicated so everyone knows the targets for improvement	There is a regular process of formal review against key performance indicators which provides the focus for discussion and exploration of innovation strategy.
(e) Innovative organization and culture	
Our organization structure does not stifle innovation but helps it to happen	Generally true and there are regular reviews and revisions to ensure this happens. In particular the provision of parallel pathways for innovation is helping.
People work well together across departmental boundaries	Increasingly necessary with the move to systems and platform products but has been the case since the 1990s when reorganization moved from a fragmented and functional approach.
There is a strong commitment to training and development of people	Has been a core principle at Hella since the early days— recruiting and training electronics specialists in the 1980s, for example. Close involvement in setting up the regional Technical School.
People are involved in suggesting ideas for improvements to products or processes	The long-running continuous improvement programmes (such as LION) have been complemented in recent years with online campaigns such as Driving E-novation.
Our structure helps us to take decisions rapidly	Although there are concerns about the speed of some processes a major review is now underway to streamline these and enable them to operate quickly whilst also offering structures for co-ordinating activities across a large global organization.
Communication is effective and works top-down, bottom-up and across the organization	Attempts are constantly being made to link what is now a large and international organization. This particularly focuses on web-based tools but there are also physical components such as regular meetings across communities of practice.

Table 5.1. *(Continued)*

Key Area	How Well Does Hella Perform?
Our reward and recognition system supports innovation	There are attempts to extend and develop non-financial incentives and to engage employees — for example, using a ramified approach to the online ideation campaigns.
We have a supportive climate for new ideas — people don't have to leave the organization to make them happen	There is general support for innovation and a recognition that the company is committed to it but also investing in it. This is evident not only in the R&D spending but also in the launch of different initiatives such as agile, Hella Ventures and the continuous improvement re-launch.
We work well in teams	Since the early days of electronics within Hella there has been a recognition of the value of cross-disciplinary integrated teams and these provide a core model for carrying innovation forward.

(f) Learning and building innovation capability

We take time to review our projects to improve our performance next time	Post-project reviews and other vehicles are in place to capture learning and improve innovation approaches. An example would be the platform strategy now being deployed in body control and customer modules where many lessons from earlier projects have been used to design the approach.
We learn from our mistakes	There is growing recognition of the need to develop more agile approaches and to allow 'intelligent failure', reviewing and improving processes for innovation on a more systematic basis.
We systematically compare our products and processes with other firms	Benchmarking and product comparison is a powerful tool for ensuring competitiveness and is widely used across the organization.
We meet and share experiences with other firms to help us learn	There is growing recognition of the value of such 'open innovation' interchange and the development of links outside the traditional automotive sector. The i-Circle model provides one such platform where experiences from different companies such

Table 5.1. *(Continued)*

Key Area	How Well Does Hella Perform?
	as Nokia, Airbus, Lufthansa and Siemens can be shared.
We are good at capturing what we have learned so that others in the organization can make use of it	Increasingly projects are piloted and then experience shared via workshops and other mechanisms to spread awareness and share good practice.
We use measurement to help identify where and when we can improve our innovation management	The company periodically reviews its innovation activities and has a number of targeted initiatives in play aimed at improving agility, participation, etc.
We learn from our periphery — we look beyond our organizational and geographical boundaries	Although there is a risk of being too closely tied to the automotive world Hella has a good track record in finding and forming valuable knowledge alliances with players outside this boundary. Most recent has been the Hella ventures operation in Silicon Valley which is specifically designed to create new connections and networks.
Experimentation is encouraged	Within key areas there is growing use of 'agile' and prototyping approaches supporting a strong investment in R&D. New models such as Hella Ventures extend this experimental and exploration capability.

EXTENDING INNOVATION CAPABILITY

So Hella has a pretty clean bill of health in terms of its innovation fitness. But as we saw at the start of the book sometimes this isn't enough. Organizations don't just need capability to manage innovation, they also need a second order capability, allowing them to step back and review their approach. They may need to emphasize some activities, reduce or even eliminate others and add new approaches to their repertoire. In short, they need the capacity for innovation model innovation.

Amongst the capabilities that might be relevant would be those additional questions outlined below. How far would it be true to say that in the ways Hella manages the 'search' question?

- *We deploy 'probe and learn' approaches to explore new directions in technologies and markets*

- *We make connections across industry to provide us with different perspectives*

- *We have mechanisms to bring in fresh perspectives — for example, recruiting from outside the industry*

- *We make regular use of formal tools and techniques to help us think 'out of the box'*

And how about its approach to innovation strategy?

- *Management create 'stretch goals' that provide the direction but not the route for innovation*

- *We actively explore the future, making use of tools and techniques like scenarios and foresight*

- *We have capacity in our strategic thinking process to challenge our current position — we think about 'how to destroy the business!'*

- *We have strategic decision-making and project selection mechanisms which can deal with more radical proposals outside of the mainstream*

- *We are not afraid to 'cannibalize' things we already do to make space for new options*

In implementing innovation how far can it say that:

- *We have alternative and parallel mechanisms for implementing and developing radical innovation projects that sit outside the 'normal' rules and procedures*

- *We have mechanisms for managing ideas that don't fit our current business — for example, we license them out or spin them off*

- *We make use of simulation, rapid prototyping tools, etc. to explore different options and delay commitment to one particular course*

- *We have strategic decision-making and project selection mechanisms which can deal with more radical proposals outside of the mainstream*

- *There is sufficient flexibility in our system for product development to allow small 'fast track' projects to happen*

In its innovation organization how true is it that:

- *Our organization allows some space and time for people to explore 'wild' ideas*

- *We have mechanisms to identify and encourage 'intrapreneurship' — if people have a good idea they don't have to leave the company to make it happen*

- *We allocate a specific resource for exploring options at the edge of what we currently do — we don't load everyone up 100%*

- *We value people who are prepared to break the rules*

- *We have high involvement from everyone in the innovation process*

- *Peer pressure creates a positive tension and creates an atmosphere to be creative*

- *Experimentation is encouraged?*

And in building effective external networks and linkages how true is it that:

- *We have extensive links with a wide range of outside sources of knowledge — universities, research centres, specialized agencies, and we actually set them up even if not for specific projects*

- *We use technology to help us become more agile and quick to pick up on and respond to emerging threats and opportunities on the periphery*

- *We have 'alert' systems to feed early warning about new trends into the strategic decision-making process*

- *We practice 'open innovation' — rich and widespread networks of contacts from whom we get a constant flow of challenging ideas*

- *We have an approach to supplier management which is open to strategic 'dalliances'*

- *We have active links into long-term research and technology community — we can list a wide range of contacts*

BUILDING REFLECTIVE CAPABILITY

Answering these questions poses questions for the ways in which Hella learns and develops its innovation capability. Successful organizations do not just recognize the importance of innovation — they understand that they need to create the context in which it can happen. And they also recognize the need to step back, reflect and review their capabilities and intervene to develop them further. So a key issue is how a company like Hella manages this strategic reflection process.

Of course, part of the answer to this has always been the role played by engaged leadership, giving a sense of clear direction and, importantly, reinforcing core values which underpin the company. Themes like entrepreneurial responsibility and the external networking strategy are good reminders of this. But how else can the theme of innovation capability be kept in the foreground and reviewed regularly?

CONVERSATIONS WITH INNOVATION

One way in which Hella has begun to create this kind of dynamic capability has been through raising the profile of discussion *about* innovation across the company. Since 2014 it has been trying to engage in a continuing reflection about it, focusing on key challenges, what could/should Hella be doing, what are other organizations doing, what could be shared across the organization as a whole? These questions form the basis of a bi-monthly gathering of senior managers from across the Hella organization in what is known as the 'i-Circle' — a forum for open and frank exploration of innovation management in the business. A mixture of presentations (both from within Hella, and from external individuals and organizations willing to share) and discussions allow for experience-sharing and mobilizing support for developing new and improved capability around innovation.

CHALLENGES ALONG THE INNOVATION FRONTIER

In the following part of the book we'll look at some of the core themes that represent key areas of challenge for any organization trying to manage innovation in the current climate. And we'll explore how Hella is adapting and extending its innovation management capability in response to these shifts.

Responding to these challenges requires new ways of innovating. Not to replace the well-established and effective routines which it already has but to extend those capabilities in new directions, to explore more of the rich innovation space out there. In particular, it needs to look at:

New dynamics — today's innovation world increasingly stresses co-creation, working with many different interacting players and users. This puts greater emphasis on prototyping and 'probe and learn' approaches, accepting failure as a part of planned experimentation and seeing it as an opportunity to learn fast.

New roles — alongside its mainstream it needs a new cast of characters on the innovation stage. Open innovation needs brokers, bridges, gatekeepers and ways of making knowledge flow. And working in the uncertain context that many emerging markets and technologies are opening up requires a much higher level of entrepreneurial thinking and behaviour. It's not just about people starting new ventures but about the mindset associated with being flexible, looking for new connections, prepared to experiment, take risks and accept failure as part of a learning process.

New structures and operating routines — making innovation happen in this new space. Uncertain environments need flexible structures that are able to move quickly and experiment.

Smart and successful large organizations are meeting this challenge by realizing that they need more than one approach to innovation. In a complex environment they try and match the variety 'out there' with multiple parallel innovation models — it's not a case of 'one size fits all'.

For example, in a recent i-Circle talk about Nokia's approach, Fabian Schlage, Innovation Manager, explained that within his company there is a core R&D-led product innovation process. And there's a user-focused group bringing in novel insights by working to co-create. There's extensive collaboration and learning via open innovation networking. Employees can become entrepreneurs, contributing their ideas and building on those across the Global Innovation Mall — a global platform across which hundreds of ideas flow every day. There's support for new ventures, firm spin offs, spinouts and spin in, venture and entrepreneurial management structures. And there's even a group with the licence to look for ways of disrupting Nokia's current business — not to destroy but working as an insurance policy to make sure they are well positioned to ride any radical new waves of change.

The good news is that Hella has a good track record in such innovation model innovation. It has grown through extending links into new worlds (open innovation), and through exploring new ways of working with Hella's core knowledge in new markets. It is trying to extend its range through investments in capabilities like the new Advanced Engineering structure (and learning to work with that) and working with internal entrepreneurs. Initiatives like 'Driving e-novation' have begun to mobilize internal ideas and entrepreneurs, and there are now moves to create further disruptive innovation capability.

Running through all of this is the need to co-ordinate many very different approaches to innovation. It's a problem sometimes called 'ambidexterity' — the ability to work in different modes simultaneously. One metaphor for this is the idea of an 'innovation orchestra'. Rather than trying to play the innovation symphony on a couple of instruments we need to bring many different instruments together, each with a different approach, playing a different part of the tune. But we also need to ensure that there is some harmony — not easy but essential if innovation is to succeed.

FURTHER RESOURCES

You can find a number of useful resources — case studies, video and audio, and tools to explore some of the themes discussed in this chapter at www.innovation-portal.info

In particular:

- Framework questions around innovation management (the Innovation Fitness Test) and for dealing with discontinuous innovation

- Video explanation of the core process model for innovation

- Case studies of organizations mapped against an innovation audit framework — 3M, Electroco, Kao, Corning, Coloplast and Cerulean

REFLECTION QUESTIONS

1. Choose an organization with which you are familiar and use the Innovation Fitness Test framework to explore how well they manage innovation.

2. Now do the same but using the Discontinuous Innovation audit framework to explore how prepared they are for disruptive external changes.

3. Innovation is a moving target — there are always new challenges on the horizon, coming from different directions. Draw a map of the threat and opportunities along the frontier of your chosen organization —technological, market, competitors, regulation, etc. — which might require new approaches to organizing and managing innovation.

NOTES

1. You can find more details of innovation challenges faced by organizations like Kodak and IBM in Joe Tidd and John Bessant (2014).

2. The IBM story is well described in Garr (2000).

3. For a more detailed discussion of 'dynamic capability' see Teece, Pisano, and Shuen (1997).

4. The Polaroid story is explored in Tripsas and Gavetti (2000).

5. This model is described in detail in Joe Tidd and John Bessant (2013).

6

MOBILISING ENTREPRENEURIAL ENGAGEMENT

Scratch under the surface of any organizations and you'll find an army of would-be entrepreneurs. People who have ideas about new products, services, processes, new business models — all sorts of interesting possibilities. They have a significant advantage over external entrepreneurs — they know the company in detail. They understand who has what particular kinds of knowledge, they have a close sense of the customers, they have a feeling for who they need to get the job done. They are, in other words, a perfect team for carrying new ventures forward.

Except that they don't. For most organizations there is a frustrating sense of sitting on top of untapped potential and for many of these employees it is equally frustrating seeing formal innovation strategy implemented but missing out on the ideas they believe could make a difference. Sometimes this frustration spills over, it starts to affect their day job and they become disaffected — in extreme cases giving up and leaving to find pastures new.

There are many reasons for unfulfilled potential of internal entrepreneurship — IE. On the part of the employees there is a risk level they are often uncomfortable with — unlike start-ups they are not necessarily prepared to bet everything on the venture — they may have family and other commitments, it may be too early in their career, they may feel uncomfortable going it alone. Plus there is the whole incentive question — why bother? In a start-up the upside of betting the family home is the chance to make a real impact and reap the rewards for all the sleepless nights and worried days. But in a corporate context the best to hope for might be a pay rise and the worst is being stifled, seeing the ideas go nowhere or someone else harvesting the benefits.

And there is a skills issue — the dream of being an entrepreneur is one thing but it's clear that having a good idea is not the same as succeeding with it. It's a craft and many would-be entrepreneurs are put off by the lack of skill. Writing business plans, securing finance and resources, pitching the idea to cynical senior managers — it's not necessarily an easy ride.

On the organization side there are some big barriers as well. First is the challenge to strategy; by its nature entrepreneurial activity is looking to find gaps, exploit cracks, push the organization in direction and places it hadn't planned. This sets up a tension — which can be healthy but often risks stifling ideas because of 'not invented here' and other effects.

Then there is the resource allocation challenge. Simply saying it wants ideas to bubble up from below is not enough — people need to be enabled to do so. And by definition if they spend time on their new ideas they won't be spending it on the projects they are supposed to be working on. Even if their ideas are worth exploring it will cost more resources to find out — develop the technology, explore the market, test the concept. So, somehow the extra resources have to be found — or cannibalized from existing budgets.

As a result, organizations and individuals wrestle with a frustrating challenge and achieve a sort of working compromise. For most of the time people do the innovative activity they are paid for, contributing in different ways to the agenda within the established strategic framework. But alongside this there is a grey area in which they are invited to push their own ideas — they contribute some extra energy, perhaps working out of hours, perhaps allowed a little time at the margin of their day job. See **Figure 6.1.**

But what if the organization tries to create a little more space and incentive? What if they recognized the untapped potential and put efforts into trying to make it happen — and taking on board the new ideas when they come through? This theme of 'intrapreneurship' is an old one but remains a challenge — and there are now some powerful new tools to help make it happen, especially using hybrid online/offline approaches across large organizations.

Let's discount the lower corner — few people involved in low impact projects — why bother?

Quadrant 2 has relatively few people involved and high impact. This is typically where groups like R&D sit, the people tasked with creating the future. They are dedicated to this and the expectation is occasional radical innovation. The good news here is that we've learned a lot about how to organize this group, how to equip them with tools and techniques, how to maximize their contribution (Chapter 13 on agile innovation, for example).

Quadrant 3 — many people involved but low impact — would be where formally mobilized continuous improvement activity sits.

Figure 6.1. A Map of Innovation Engagement.

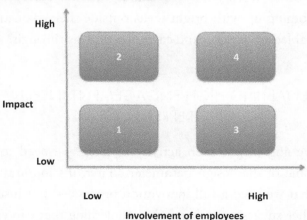

This is essentially high involvement innovation of a 'do what we do but better' kind, focused on a clear strategic target and incremental in nature. And it is where we've made a lot of progress in innovation management — learning how to enable and support people in contributing innovation as part of their daily working lives.[1]

This is powerful because whilst each innovative idea may be simple and have a relatively low impact the cumulative effects can be significant. Toyota's position as the world's most productive carmaker stems not from some specialist expertise or equipment but from a decades long commitment to mobilizing its workforce in kaizen — continuous incremental improvement.[2] Hella's own experience during the tough 'Lopez era' where pressures from key customers for cost reduction and performance improvement were a real challenge underlines the power of mobilizing continuous improvement of this kind. (We discuss this theme in more detail in Chapter 7.)

The interesting space is the fourth cell — where we have many people involved but we're also looking for radical, unexpected higher impact innovation. How do we target and enable this in our organizations — and how can we migrate from the CI low impact to build on some of the more radical ideas from there as well. In other words, how to enable internal entrepreneurship, people coming up with bright ideas outside their mainstream and being enabled to develop and carry those ideas through?

ENABLING HIGH ENGAGEMENT INTERNAL ENTREPRENEURSHIP

If we're going to put such activity in place we need to be clear about some of the design parameters. First, it's important to recognize that we need a full innovation process — not just mobilizing another suggestion scheme, but something that can enable the transit from ideas to value creating reality.

Figure 6.2. Simplified Model of the Innovation Process.

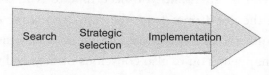

For this we need a process with at least three key elements:

1. Ideation — sourcing ideas

2. Selection — choosing which to back

3. Implementation — carrying them forward down the road from 'gleam in the eye' to fully functioning and value creating

Figure 6.2 gives an example of this.

We already know how to do this in quadrant 2 — the specialist tracks for 'professionals' in the innovation game such as R&D, production engineering or systems development. And we have a similar, simpler model for continuous improvement — high involvement incremental innovation is about short cycles of finding a problem, generating ideas to solve it, choosing one, implementing, reviewing a repeat.

What about the high involvement entrepreneur zone — how can we build a model for these three phases there? It's clear that we need a systematic approach — not just a cosmetic one-off, otherwise we risk not being taken seriously. And we need to replicate the whole innovation process — not just the front-end ideation. How can we do it? A good place to start would be by reviewing experience in the other zones of our model and adapting elements of those initiatives.

Ideation — Once Upon a Time …

Imagine you have a workforce who enthusiastically take up your challenge and begin to suggest ideas. You employ a 100 people and after week one your suggestion box is full of 100 ideas; not all of them will be great and you need time to read through them and sift out the good ones from the rest. And some of the good ones will require a lot more effort and input from other people to make them happen. You're also conscious of the need to acknowledge all the ideas and give people an update on what you will do with them. All of this takes time — so you find yourself at the end of week two still struggling to process, choose, act on and report on the first batch of ideas. But another 100 come through the box, and next week another hundred .... So that by the end of the month you are drowning in ideas, unable to respond and also not doing all the other things you are supposed to be doing to keep the business going. Idea management has become your fulltime occupation.

Outside the employees are getting restive — all the ideas they've put in and what has come out? Some begin to think that it's not worth suggesting anything because no one is listening, they're not doing anything with the wonderful new initiatives offered to them.

Pretty soon the flood of ideas slows to a trickle — making your task more manageable but actually reflecting the fading out of interest in the whole process. And rather than a slow death the model just fades away into the background.

What Went Wrong?

- No capacity to organize and manage the ideas
- No feedback on progress
- No clear pathway for further implementation
- No clear selection criteria — people think you just back pet ideas
- No transparency — the closed box problem
- No resources for further implementation

- No management of the idea process — no dedicated resource
- No direction, a reverse blunderbuss approach

Not surprisingly the effort is likely to fail. Not from a lack of commitment to its principles, either from leadership or from employees, both of whom see its potential value. Not because of a lack of ideas — the problem is the reverse. It fails because of a lack of a system to enable it to happen. Just as the dedicated teams in R&D or business development have a pathway and process to enable the movement of ideas to value, so the organization needs something to manage high involvement innovation. And by its nature the channels and mechanisms for doing this can't be the dedicated specialist tracks — it needs a new route.

Part of the solution is to take the simple ideas and close the loop fast. Feedback support to the people who suggested them and allow them to implement them. That has several benefits — it's fast, they get feedback, they feel a sense of autonomy, they can influence and change their workplace. And this model works well in CI programmes where we are mostly dealing with many suggestions for incremental improvement innovations.

Having lots of ideas to manage can be helped if we organize them quickly into categories based on implement-ability. If they are small and simple, just do it. The consequence of this is that we can get a high volume of incremental improvements that can be implemented fast — essentially the basis of a good kaizen system. Systems like this still need organizing but if we set the boundaries around the problem as requiring simple, easy to implement ideas then we can get high frequency short cycle innovation.

Where this model breaks down is when we need to explore bigger ideas. Ideas with more potential impact but which may take other resources to implement. Ideas which need time and perhaps a different perspective to review. Ideas which also might benefit from polishing, modifying, refining.

Going Underground

An alternative approach is to encourage bootlegging and below the radar experimentation, relying on natural energy and the dynamics of teamwork to come up with ideas, argue about them and select, refine and put their energies into making them happen. 3M is a company famous for this approach — it has worked hard to create a culture of 'intrapreneurship' in which motivated employees go beyond their job (and very often way beyond their normal working hours) and function like a start-up. They work on their idea, solving problems, finding resources, refining and testing until it is robust enough to present to the company for possible approval and further support.

3M have worked hard over many years to perfect the system, creating an infrastructure which supports these intrapreneurs — for example with access to 'venture finance', with the possibility of getting some formal time and resource to take the project further if the initial pitch is successful. It rides on the motivation of frustration, perceived new opportunity for the individuals, autonomy and intrinsic motivation — but it also benefits from external support. 3M can look to great success stories like PostIt Notes as the results of such an intrapreneurship approach.

This model works, just as the CI one does — but both of them are stepping stones in **Figure 6.1**, moving towards the goal of high involvement, high entrepreneurship innovation. The challenges posed by the 3M route are essentially about taking an informal social process and making it more widely available. In particular:

• Getting more people involved

• Drawing in wider cross-functional perspectives rather than the 'local' team of friends

• Exposing the ideas to the wider community to add and help shape it

- Engaging a wider set of people to contribute energy and resources

- Providing the management and facilitation to help this to happen

Jumping on the Platform ...

A third option is emerging that begins to bridge these two worlds and, importantly, one which offers a complete innovation system rather than just the ideation front end. This uses online collaboration platforms with increasingly high levels of functionality.

Back in 1714 the British Navy faced a problem — they kept losing their ships. Whilst they were able to build and sail some of the finest vessels in the world, and use them to defend a growing empire around the world, they were unable to tell at a given point in time exactly where they were. That was embarrassing for the gentlemen in the Admiralty but much more serious for the captains and crew actually on the ships; not being able to navigate exposed them to all kinds of danger. A number of tragic accidents resulted, in one case involving an entire fleet of ships running aground on rocks as they tried to return home to the safety of Plymouth harbour.

The reason for this concern was simple; whilst it was possible to measure latitude accurately the same was not true of longitude, and without the two it was impossible to 'fix' a ship's position. The problem lay in the simple fact that there were no reliable clocks available that could be carried on board. In response to this growing challenge the British Parliament passed the Longitude Act which established an innovation contest, putting up a prize of £20,000 (which in today's money would be worth around €3m), to be awarded to anyone who could build a reliable portable chronometer. The winner, after a long search, was a man called John Harrison and his design is still to be seen in the Royal Naval Museum in London.

Across the Channel in 1869 the French Army had a similar concern, this time to do with provisioning troops for long marches. Their challenge lay in finding a substitute for butter, which had a tendency to go rancid after a few days; once again the problem became the focus for another innovation contest with a prize of 12,000 francs (about €150,000 today). The winner in this case was Hippolyte Mège-Mouriès, the man who gave the world margarine, a product still found in various forms on supermarket shelves today. He was following in glorious footsteps — the contest had originally been set up by Emperor Louis Napoleon 3rd in 1795 as an annual attempt to draw out good ideas — another notable winner in 1809 was Nicolas Appert who invented the world's first food canning process.

These examples highlight a challenge in innovation. It's all about turning ideas to value — and it makes sense at the 'fuzzy front end' to open up the challenge of idea suggestion to as many people as possible. The trouble is that organizing innovation contests to do that takes a great deal of effort in attracting ideas, organizing them and making decisions about them. In the past this meant you needed a sponsor at the level of the king of England or the emperor of France and a whole organization working for them to run the contest.

But not any more. With the widespread availability of internet platforms has come a new world of innovation competitions in which many ideas can be quickly sourced around a focused challenge. More important, others can join in adding their comments and support, so that a community can be built around the ideas. And others can help with the evaluation, using the 'wisdom of crowds' to help arrive at good decisions about which ideas to support and develop further. As we gain experience in running innovation contests so they have matured into powerful platforms, a valuable addition to our innovation toolkit.

Their history goes back to the early days of automating the suggestion box — essentially they made it possible for many people to input ideas and get some acknowledgement and feedback on their status. As a fast collection of ideas they worked fine but the real benefits began to emerge when they could help with the idea management process — choosing and developing ideas and keeping people updated on progress.

Innovation management software of this kind rapidly matured, with a number of modules added to give the kind of functionality we were looking for in the above discussion.[3] Typically today's platforms offer support for:

a. *Finding ideas* ....

o Ideation support — open gateway for people to contribute their ideas

o Database to store and keep track of all ideas submitted

o Comment facility so others can add their responses and reactions — a kind of 'Facebook' 'like' and comment feature

o Shared idea development in which different comments can be used to refine and improve the idea

o Grouping — so that ideas (and the people suggesting them) can be linked together

b. *Selecting ideas*

o Giving users of the system a chance to rate and evaluate ideas, again both with simple scores and with comments and refinements

o Engaging multiple perspectives — for example evaluation by users, by experts of various kinds and even by 'investors' — people with notional money to invest who help manage a 'stock market' for ideas

o Feedback and status — transparency so that everyone can see what is going on and what happened to their ideas, where they are in the process

c. *Implementing ideas*
   o Providing online meeting places where teams can take their ideas further forward and develop them for full evaluation

   o Offline support for teams to work up their ideas

   o Online and offline pitching events at which ideas are judged and decisions about formal backing and support are taken

d. *Targeting ideation*
   o Using campaigns of various kinds to target and focus ideation along key strategic directions

e. *Knowledge management*
   o Capturing and synthesizing all information from the platform and looking for patterns, mining for linkages, helping redeploy the knowledge held within and across the organization

PERFORMING ON THE PLATFORM

Powerful though the software is, the key issue with such platforms remains how they are actually implemented. Experience suggests that getting the best out of these powerful tools doesn't happen by accident — it's a learning process in which capability is gradually built and embedded. It's not a case of automating innovation but rather of learning to use tools more precisely. And it underlines the need to keep people in the equation — and at key points to enable 'off-line' physical interaction as well as online collaboration.

We can imagine a simple staircase model through which organizations learn to use collaboration platforms effectively (**Table 6.1**).

DEALING WITH THE CHALLENGES IN INTERNAL ENTREPRENEURSHIP

Drawing the threads of the above discussion together it is clear that there is significant potential opportunity in mobilizing

Table 6.1. Characteristics of Collaboration Platforms for Innovation.

Level	Characteristics
1. Simple front end ideation	Automating the suggestion box, providing a mechanism to 'crowd-source' ideas and collect them
2. Interactive front end	Engaging other people in reviewing, refining, commenting on ideas
3. Targeted interactive front end	Using targeted campaigns and challenges to draw out ideas in a particular direction of strategic importance. Requires an 'owner'/sponsor of the challenge
4. Ideation and judgement	Adds in possibility for others to evaluate and judge, contribute to selection of 'good' ideas. Can bring in specialist/expert judges. Also possibility of 'investors' — mobilizing 'idea markets' to get a sense of which ideas achieve popular support
5. Building communities of practice	Enables teams to form and interact in the further development of their ideas after selection in the early rounds. May involve offline/physical meeting to develop ideas. May involve training inputs of various kinds to help strengthen the core idea and make it ready for 'pitching' in final selection rounds.
6. Connection to mainstream innovation system	Involves some kind of 'pitch' of entrepreneurial idea to senior managers who will select and allocate development resources to take the idea forward. At this point the team may be augmented with specialists to help move the idea forward. The results are measured using organization KPIs and reward systems linked to those.
7. Integration into the innovation system	This pattern of innovation becomes part of the culture, running in parallel with other activities. Knowledge is captured and stored, re-used to support new targeted campaigns and recombined creatively.
8. Extension to players outside the organization	Mobilizing the model to bring in suppliers, users and others as part of co-creation infrastructure

internal entrepreneurship. But it won't happen by accident or by simply putting a platform in place. Instead there are some key innovation management routines that need to be explored and embedded.

First, as we've seen, is idea management — it is hard enough in continuous improvement programmes to deal with lots of ideas in a systematic fashion and there we are only concerned with refinements along established trajectories. Evaluating bigger and more complex ideas soon becomes a challenge as the volume of suggestions grows. But platforms have started to help — not only can we capture but we can also refine and build on ideas. And there is the added advantage of being able to store and re-use ideas, helping to ratchet the gains from encouraging front-end ideas.

And we can also solve the judgment issue — instead of relying on senior managers to evaluate and approve ideas we now can build selection and evaluation into the platform. Using 'the wisdom of crowds' can spread the load of judging ideas and providing some important early stage filtering. Evaluating ideas can include other elements like idea markets in which notional investors rate ideas. And there is still scope for expert judges. The emerging technology of idea contests means that the barriers associated with a slow evaluation and feedback process can be lowered, at least at the early stages.

A second issue is time and resource allocation. Some organizations use an umbrella figure to indicate to staff that they have 'permission to play' with a proportion of their time — for example, at 3M it is 15%, Google 20%. But behind that is the assumption that employees put in more of their own time — they match it with their efforts. This is always a tricky issue because there is a cost to allowing this time — but, equally, without giving people some slack they won't be able to innovate. So how do you signal the opportunity and create enough space for them to follow through?

Once again there is some helpful learning from platforms and idea contests — in the early stages it is almost a game, something people can put their spare time into. Because it is early stage and conceptual we are not talking about huge amounts of investment but nonetheless there is a filter which only lets serious players through. They can form teams and networks to share the load and some kind of incentive, both personal and organizational, is important — their idea, if it wins, will be rewarded not just instrumentally but by being listened to and taken further. So, gradually we can widen the funnel at the front end of innovation and allow novel concepts to emerge.

A third challenge and an interesting point comes where the transition occurs from online teamwork to physically working together, refining and polishing ideas to a point where they can be judged. For the organization this represents a commitment of time to allow employees to work up their ideas, and from senior management to give them a hearing. And there is also the skills issue — how do employees turn into entrepreneurs? They need training in some of the basic themes around preparing a business case, financial planning, etc.

As the winning ideas take shape and become firm innovation project proposals so there is an increasing need for support to help them grow, but, at the same time, bring them more closely in line with the organization's mainstream rules for innovation project resource allocation. Incubating early stage ideas and providing the mentoring and training need to help them grow is an important part of the later stages of platform working.[4]

WHY THIS IS IMPORTANT FOR HELLA

Despite many formal channels for mobilizing innovation across the company, Hella — in common with many large organizations — faces the challenge of not always being able to tap into the ideas of their workforce. The principle of doing so is embedded deeply in the corporate value of entrepreneurial responsibility — but the question is how to enable it? The problem is compounded by the fact that the company is so busy innovating along its mainstream pathways, delivering a steady stream of product and process innovations that are part of the overall strategic plan.

A desire to unlock the latent entrepreneurship of a larger part of the workforce is not only about sourcing good ideas. It is also about offering a route for employees to explore and channel their frustrations — giving a sense of being able to shape the future of a business operating in a very challenging landscape. Associated with this is the risk that some of those employees might eventually leave the organization through frustration, a sense of not being heard, of their ideas not being valued.

The challenge presents itself as one of how to encourage some wider front-end thinking? But also how to execute on those ideas? How to build a culture of self-motivated innovation, strategically targeted and driven forward by internal entrepreneurs with a passion for change?

As we've seen there is increasing experience around using collaboration platforms to help with this. The experience of other large players such as Nokia, Siemens and Airbus (all of whom shared their experiences at various i-Circle meetings) suggests that there are significant opportunities in this approach and that it can not only provide motivation but also a stream of useful new ideas for the business. Importantly, it can also build communities and mobilize the internal knowledge base, helping to spread and re-deploy the deep competence base within the organization.

HELLA'S RESPONSE TO THE CHALLENGE ...

Back in 2014 Hella GE launched the first version of a contest which attracted a great deal of interest and drew ideas from across the company. The model was typical — a short sprint process spread over a few months during which teams were invited to form and suggest ideas for new developments which would be of value to the company. Others were involved in judging those ideas, both as experts and also as 'investors' acting like a venture capital market placing bets on the ideas that seemed most promising. The ideas were gradually whittled down to a short list of teams who made 'pitches' to senior management at an Innovation Day held at Nurburgring. The real prize wasn't the day out or the rewards for the winning team; it was being able to take those ideas forward to the next stage of development as part of the company's project portfolio.

Overall, 800 employees participated in interdisciplinary teams across the organization. They generated 132 ideas which were refined into 60 Business Cases for further evaluation. The top 10 were transferred into Advanced Engineering and there were three overall winners.

Driving E-novation was valuable not just for drawing out some novel ideas from across the company; it catalyzed creativity and showed how big an appetite there was for thinking about innovation possibilities. But it also offered a laboratory for learning about how to use this powerful new innovation tool. How to communicate the core challenge, how to attract participants, how to keep people informed, how to run the selection rounds — and how to maintain momentum after the contest has finished?

In particular, one of the issues it surfaced was a common experience amongst companies employing innovation contests — the challenge of innovation isn't just one of sourcing new ideas but also of progressing them to the point where they can generate value. The principles are the same — how to harness the creativity across the company — but the focus shifts to one of accelerating ideas to value.

That was the underlying theme of Driving E-novation 2, a second contest building on the experience of the first and trying to focus and align more effectively with the other innovation activities in the company.

Driving E-Novation 2 — Getting into the Fast Lane

The focus of the new challenge is, as the name suggests, getting additional momentum behind good ideas. Where the first contest had generated ideas that found their way into the Advanced Engineering portfolio, this second thrust intended to accelerate projects from within that portfolio through bringing new thinking to bear.

Importantly, it is recognized that not every expert works within the electronics division so this contest spread the net more widely to mobilize ideas from across the company. The target was to stimulate entrepreneurship and collaboration, and to deliver something of value through implementation in the near future.

The timeline and goals of the contest were clear and challenging; from a launch in March 2016 it would run live until the end of May with a final review event at the end of June. The winners would receive an additional budget and other resources together with a mentor to help them take their ideas forward.

Drawing on lessons from the first contest the basic structure involved a series of rounds during which ideas could be refined and elaborated. Three different groups were involved:

- 'talents' — people with ideas and knowledge

- 'entrepreneurs' — teams drawing on those talents to carry forward ideas to accelerate transfer to business

- 'investors' — experts ('power investors') and others ('community investors') who supported, judged and helped rank the ideas through investing virtual money

The net was cast widely across the company and attracted a great deal of interest and activity from very diverse areas. Altogether 1,276 people registered to use the platform, made up of:

- 29 entrepreneurs (representing 31 'ventures')

- 135 Power investors and 477 Community investors

- 633 talents

The process involved an intensive effort across the platform and eventually led to nine finalists presenting their ideas at a session hosted by Porsche in Leipzig. Of those, three winning ideas were selected to go forward with full support.

Importantly, this contest was trying to source new thinking to accelerate projects already in the portfolio. For example, one of the winning ideas offers a new route solving a big problem in car security by combining two lines of work already going on within the company. The idea has great promise and practicality both in terms of offering a low cost solution and doing so rapidly; the aim is to have the product in volume production by 2020.

The motivation for venture teams is fairly direct but it is interesting that some of the other participants also valued the experience. For example, one of the winning' investors' felt that it offered him an opportunity to participate in shaping Hella's thinking about its product portfolio at a time when so much is changing in disruptive fashion.

Lessons Learned for Future Capability Building

Overall, some key lessons emerged for Hella about the role and value of innovation competitions like this:

- It offers a way of drawing people together from across a large and diverse company, and focuses their thinking and efforts in key innovation challenges
- The 'game' approach helps motivate and sustain participation
- The different roles help build a culture of entrepreneurship across GE and the wider organization
- And it is a powerful focusing tool for action — the winning projects have already kicked off and first revenues are expected in 2019–2020

FURTHER RESOURCES

You can find a number of useful resources — case studies, video and audio, and tools to explore some of the themes discussed in this chapter at www.innovation-portal.info

In particular:

- Case studies of organizations using collaboration platforms to extend their internal entrepreneurship options — Liberty Global, Airbus, Lufthansa Systems, Wilo, Nokia

- A framework maturity model for high involvement innovation and an assessment template

REFLECTION QUESTIONS

1. Look at cases of others working on this theme of internal entre-preneurship and the different ways in which they are trying to enable this. What factors are important in making such systems work and what lessons would you take to apply to other organizations?

2. If you were appointed to advise a large organization like Hella:
   ○ What would you recommend?
   ○ What problems can you see downstream?

3. Use the high involvement innovation assessment framework (on the Innovation Portal above) to carry out a review of an organization of your choice and their level of maturity in build-ing such capability

NOTES

1. For more on this theme of internal entrepreneurship see Gundling (2000) and Iyer and Davenport (2008).

2. For more detailed discussion of continuous improvement approaches see Bessant (2003), Imai (1997), Boer, Berger, Chapman and Gertsen (1999), and Schroeder and Robinson (2004).

3. For a more extensive discussion of the ways in which platforms and online markets can support innovation see Bessant and Moeslein (2011), Harhoff and Lakhani (2016) and Reichwald et al., (2013).

4. For a more extensive discussion of the element underpinning mature capability in such collaboration platforms see John Bessant (2017).

7

THE CHALLENGE OF CONTINUOUS IMPROVEMENT

In an uncertain world there's a real need to mobilize as much effort behind the innovation task as possible. And one of the great opportunities for doing so is to engage the creativity of all employees in the organization. As one manager memorably put it, the big benefit of this approach is that *'with every pair of hands you get a free brain!'* It's a paradox today that we have the key resource of creativity fitted as standard equipment in every person we employ — yet many organizations fail to recognize or manage to tap into this. One of the fathers of modern quality management thinking, Joseph Juran, used to call this *'the gold in the mine'* — our challenge is finding up-to-date and effective ways to extract this mineral![1]

Of course, this is simple enough to say but hard to achieve in practice — high involvement innovation of this kind isn't as easy as it sounds. In principle, everyone can be creative and has plenty of ideas for improving things within the organization. But enabling them to do so — and sustaining their involvement — depends on creating an environment in which that behaviour can flourish.

The idea that people can contribute to innovation through suggesting and implementing their ideas isn't new. Attempts to utilize this approach in a formal way can be traced back to the

18th Century, when the 8th shogun Yoshimune Tokugawa introduced the suggestion box in Japan. In 1871 Denny's shipyard in
Dumbarton, Scotland, employed a programme of incentives to
encourage suggestions about productivity-improving techniques;
they sought to draw out *'any change by which work is rendered
either superior in quality or more economical in cost'*. In 1894 the
National Cash Register company made considerable efforts to
mobilize the *'hundred — headed brain'* which their staff represented, whilst the Lincoln Electric Company started implementing
an 'incentive management system' in 1915. NCR's ideas, especially
around suggestion schemes, found their way back to Japan where
the textile firm of Kanebuchi Boseki introduced them in 1905.[2]

Back in the 1940s the Chief Executive of 3M highlighted well
the leadership challenge in putting such systems in place:

> *As our business grows, it becomes increasingly necessary
> to delegate responsibility and to encourage men and
> women to exercise their initiative. This requires consider-
> able tolerance. Those men and women, to whom we dele-
> gate authority and responsibility, if they are good people,
> are going to want to do their jobs in their own way.*

> *Mistakes will be made. But if a person is essentially right,
> the mistakes he or she makes are not as serious in the long
> run as the mistakes management will make if it undertakes
> to tell those in authority exactly how they must do their
> jobs.*

> *Management that is destructively critical when mistakes
> are made kills initiative. It's essential that we have many
> people with initiative if we are to continue to grow.*

Although the ideas were well-established a century ago it was
particularly in post-war Japan and the 'quality revolution' that we
saw their emergence as a systemic approach to enabling continuous improvement. Manufacturing businesses there seemed able to

manage the process of delivering customer value through speed, flexibility, quality and with high productivity. Inevitably, attention focussed on how these gains were being achieved — and it became clear that a fundamentally different model of organizing manufacturing had been evolving.

Early attempts to emulate the Japanese experience often failed. For example, the widespread adoption of quality circles in the late 1970s often led to short-term gains and then gradual disillusionment and abandonment of the schemes later.[3] In large measure this can be attributed to a mistaken belief in there being a single transferable solution to the problem of quality which Western firms had to try and acquire. The reality was, of course, that the 'Japanese' model involved a completely different philosophy of organizing and managing production.

This became increasingly clear as Western firms began to explore other dimensions of Japanese practice — for example, their approach to production scheduling, to inventory control, to flow, to maintenance and to flexibility.[4] The emergent model was one in which people were treated as a key part of the solution to the problems of production — and as a problem-finding and solving resource for dealing with new ones. In order to mobilize this potential it was necessary to invest in training, and the more widely this was done, the more flexibly people could be used across a manufacturing facility. Having trained staff with the capability of finding and solving problems, it made sense to pass the responsibility for much of the operational decision-making to them, so workers became involved in quality, in maintenance, in production scheduling and smoothing, etc. And in order to maximize the flexibility associated with devolution of decision-making new forms of work organization, especially based around team-working made sense.

There is nothing peculiarly Japanese in any of these concepts — rather, they simply represent a re-integration of tasks and responsibilities which had been systematically fragmented and separated

off by the traditions of the factory system in the 19th Century and
Ford/Taylor style mass production in the 20th. Nonetheless, the
gap which had opened up was significant, and was highlighted in
particular by a series of studies of the world automobile industry
in the late 1980s.

From detailed studies of productivity of car assembly plants
around the world it became clear that Japanese operated plants
were significantly better performers across a range of dimensions.
Efforts to identify the source of these significant advantages
revealed that the major differences lay not in higher levels of capital investment or more modern equipment, but in the ways in
which production was organized and managed.[5]

The same pattern emerged in many other sectors — for example, Schroeder and Robinson reported that Japanese firms received
around 37.4 ideas per employee, coming from around 80% of the
workforce and with nearly 90% of these being implemented. And
growing understanding of the underlying principles led to the
emergence and diffusion of the concept of 'lean' thinking.

SO WHAT IS 'CONTINUOUS IMPROVEMENT' (CI)?

The underlying principle of continuous improvement is clear and
well expressed in a Japanese phrase — *'best is the enemy of better'*.
Rather than assuming that a single 'big hit' change will deal with
the elimination of waste and the causes of defects, CI involves a
long-term systematic attack on the problem. A metaphor for this is
the gradual wearing down of stone through the continuous drip-
ping of water on to it from above — it doesn't happen overnight
but the cumulative effect is as effective as a powerful drill.

Basically CI involves high levels of participation in predomi-
nantly incremental innovation focused particularly on process
improvement. CI is deceptively simple; its power comes from sustained and widespread commitment to this approach. And it is

important not to dismiss it as small in scale; research evidence consistently shows that most innovation, most of the time, is doing what we do a little better. CI accounts for the vast majority of innovation effort — less than 10% is really radical or disruptive. And the big advantage of CI is that such incremental innovation builds on what we already know, it is lower in risk and faster to implement than radical change.

Over the years a wide range of tools have been developed to enable CI but at its heart it is a simple engine for finding and solving problems systematically. A famous version of this is the 'Deming Wheel', named after the US quality engineer who first developed it.[6] Another is the 'plan-do-check-act' cycle which provides a focus for systematic incremental innovation.

CHALLENGES IN MAKING CI HAPPEN

CI looks like an attractive option for any organization — but making it happen depends on a sustained and organized effort. It involves a journey towards a destination in which people naturally find and solve problems and contribute their innovation efforts. It's not a simple 'plug and play' solution; experience suggests that it requires careful attention to building and embedding new behaviours within the organization and this process takes time.

A major research programme during the late 1990s looked at this challenge across many countries and their key finding was that high involvement innovation (HII) is not a binary thing, an on-off switch.[7] It needs to become a core part of the culture — 'the way we do things around here' if it is to have a sustained impact and become a strategic resource. And that depends on building nine core capabilities:

- Establish high involvement innovation as a core value — the belief that little improvements from everyone do matter

- Recognition and reward — this core value is reinforced by relevant incentives (and this is less about money than about being listened to, empowered, enabled to contribute)

- Training and development to give people the skills to be an effective innovator

- Establishing a core process to enable continuous improvement to happen — including allowing time and space for it to operate

- Idea management systems which give feedback and action to ideas

- Facilitation and support for it — coaching, training, structures, etc.

- Leadership — creating the context in which HII can happen, and leading by example — 'walking the talk'

- Strategic direction — clear guidance about where and why improvements matter and 'policy deployment' to communicate this clearly

- Building dynamic capability — continuously reviewing and updating the HII approach

In particular, the research suggests that we can think of an evolutionary process, moving through a number of levels — and there is no guarantee that organizations will progress to the next level. Moving on means having to find ways of overcoming the particular obstacles associated with different stages.

At the first stage — level 1 — there is little, if any, CI activity going on, and when it does happen it is essentially random in nature and occasional in frequency. People do help to solve problems from time to time but there is no formal attempt to mobilize or build on this activity, and many organizations may actively restrict the opportunities for it to take place. The normal state is one in which CI is not looked for, not recognized, not supported — and often, not even noticed. Not surprisingly, there is little impact associated with this kind of change.

Level 2 involves setting up a formal process for finding and solving problems in a structured and systematic way — and training and encouraging people to use it. Supporting this will be some form of reward/recognition arrangement to motivate and encourage continued participation. Ideas will be managed through some form of system for processing and progressing as many as possible, and handling those which cannot be implemented. Underpinning the whole set-up will be an infrastructure of appropriate mechanisms (teams, task forces or whatever), facilitators and some form of steering group to enable CI to take place, and to monitor and adjust its operation over time. None of this can happen without top management support and commitment of resources to back that up.

Level 2 certainly contributes improvements but these may lack focus and are often concentrated at a local level, having minimal impact on more strategic concerns of the organization. The danger is that, once having established the habit of CI, it may lack any clear target and begin to fall away. In order to maintain progress there is a need to move to the next level of CI — concerned with strategic focus and systematic improvement.

Level 3 involves coupling the CI habit to the strategic goals of the organization such that all the various local level improvement activities of teams and individuals can be aligned. In order to do this two key behaviours need to be added to the basic suite — those of strategy deployment and of monitoring and measuring. Strategy (or policy) deployment involves communicating the overall strategy of the organization and breaking it down into manageable objectives towards which CI activities in different areas can be targeted. Linked to this is the need to learn to monitor and measure the performance of a process and use this to drive the continuous improvement cycle.

Level 3 activity represents the point at which CI makes a significant impact on the bottom line — for example in reducing throughput times, scrap rates, excess inventory, etc. It is particularly effective in conjunction with efforts to achieve external measurable standards (such as ISO 9000) where the disciplines of monitoring and measurement provide drivers for eliminating variation and tracking down root cause problems. The majority of 'success stories' in CI can be found at this level — but it is not the end of the journey.

One of the limits of level 3 CI is that the direction of activity is still largely set by management and within prescribed limits. Activities may take place at different levels, from individuals through small groups to cross-functional teams, but they are still largely responsive and steered externally. The move to level 4 introduces a new element — that of 'empowerment' of individuals and groups to experiment and innovate on their own initiative.

Clearly, this is not a step to be taken lightly, and there are many situations where it would be inappropriate — for example, where established procedures are safety critical. But the principle of 'internally directed' CI as opposed to externally steered activity is important, since it allows for the open-ended learning behaviour we normally associate with professional research scientists and engineers. It requires a high degree of understanding of, and commitment to, the overall strategic objectives, together with training to a high level to enable effective experimentation.

Level 5 is a notional end-point for the journey — a condition where everyone is fully involved in experimenting and improving things, in sharing knowledge and in creating the complete learning organization. Table 7.1 illustrates the key elements in each stage:

LEARNING CONTINUOUS IMPROVEMENT

Moving along this journey is not a matter of time serving or even of resources — though without resources it is unlikely that things will get far any more than a car without petrol can be expected to.

Table 7.1. Stages in the Evolution of CI Capability.

Stage of Development	Typical Characteristics
(1) 'Natural'/background CI	Random problem-solving No formal efforts or structure Occasional bursts punctuated by inactivity and nonparticipation Dominant mode of problem-solving is by specialists Short-term benefits No strategic impact
(2) Structured CI	Formal attempts to create and sustain CI Use of a formal problem-solving process Use of participation Training in basic CI tools Structured idea management system Recognition system Often parallel system to operations
(3) Goal-oriented CI	All of the above, plus formal deployment of strategic goals Monitoring and measurement of CI against these goals In-line system
(4) Proactive/empowered CI	All of the above, plus responsibility for mechanisms, timing, etc., devolved to problem-solving unit Internally directed rather than externally directed CI High levels of experimentation
(5) Full CI capability — the learning organization	CI as the dominant way of life Automatic capture and sharing of learning Everyone actively involved in innovation process Incremental and radical innovation

But the essence of progress along the CI road is *learning* — acquiring, practising and repeating behaviours until they become ingrained as 'the way we do things round here' — the culture of the organization.

The basic behaviour patterns or routines which have to be learned are outlined in Table 7.2.

Learning these behaviours begins with moving to a new level and then involves extensive broadening out and modifying within

Table 7.2. Behavioural Patterns in Continuous Improvement.

Ability	Constituent Behaviours
'Getting the CI habit' — developing the ability to generate sustained involvement in CI	• people make use of some formal problem-finding and solving cycle • people use appropriate simple tools and techniques to support CI • people begin to use simple measurement to shape the improvement process • people (as individuals and/or groups) initiate and carry through CI activities — they participate in the process • ideas are responded to in a clearly defined and timely fashion — either implemented or otherwise dealt with • managers support the CI process through allocation of time, money, space and other resources • managers recognize informal (but not necessarily financial) ways the contribution of employees to CI • managers lead by example, becoming actively involved in design and implementation of CI • managers support experiment by not punishing mistakes but by encouraging learning from them
'Focusing CI' — generating and sustaining the ability to link CI activities to the strategic goals of the company	• individuals and groups use the organization's strategic goals and objectives to focus and prioritize improvements • everyone understands (i.e. is able to explain) what the company's or department's strategy, goals and objectives are

Table 7.2. (*Continued*)

Ability	Constituent Behaviours
	• individuals and groups (e.g. departments, CI teams) assess their proposed changes (before embarking on initial investigation and implementing a solution) against departmental or company objectives to ensure they are consistent with them
	• individuals and groups monitor/measure the results of their improvement activity and the impact it has on strategic or departmental objectives
	• CI activities are an integral part of the individual or groups work, not a parallel activity
'Spreading the word' — generating the ability to move CI activity across organizational boundaries	• people co-operate across internal divisions (e.g. cross-functional groups) in CI as well as working in their own areas
	• people understand and share an holistic view (process understanding and ownership)
	• people are oriented towards internal and external customers in their CI activity
	• specific CI projects with outside agencies — customers, suppliers, etc. — are taking place
	• relevant CI activities involve representatives from different organizational levels
'Continuous improvement of continuous improvement' — generating the ability to strategically manage the development of CI	• the CI system is continually monitored and developed; a designated individual or group monitors the CI system and measures the incidence (i.e. frequency and location) of CI activity and the results of CI activity
	• there is a cyclical planning process whereby (a) the CI system is regularly reviewed and, if necessary, amended (single-loop learning)

Table 7.2. (*Continued*)

Ability	Constituent Behaviours
	• there is periodic review of the CI system in relation to the organization as a whole, which may lead to a major regeneration (double-loop learning)
	• senior management make available sufficient resources (time, money, personnel) to support the ongoing development of the CI system.
	• ongoing assessment ensures that the organization's structure and infrastructure and the CI system consistently support and reinforce each other
	• the individual/group responsible for designing the CI system design it to fit within the current structure and infrastructure
	• individuals with responsibility for particular company processes/systems hold ongoing reviews to assess whether these processes/systems and the CI system remain compatible
	• people with responsibility for the CI system ensure that when a major organizational change is planned its potential impact on the CI system is assessed and adjustments are made as necessary
'Walking the talk' — generating the ability to articulate and demonstrate CI values	• the 'management style' reflects commitment to CI values
	• when something goes wrong the natural reaction of people at all levels is to look for reasons why, etc. rather than to blame individual(s)
	• people at all levels demonstrate a shared belief in the value of small steps and that everyone can contribute, by themselves, and are actively involved in making and recognizing incremental improvements

Table 7.2. *(Continued)*

Ability	Constituent Behaviours
'The learning organization' — generating the ability to learn through CI activity	• everyone learns from their experiences, both positive and negative
	• individuals seek out opportunities for learning/personal development (e.g. actively experiment, set their own learning objectives)
	• individuals and groups at all levels share (make available) their learning from *all* work experiences
	• the organization articulates and consolidates (captures and shares) the learning of individuals and groups
	• managers accept and, where necessary, act on all the learning that takes place
	• people and teams ensure that their learning is captured by making use of the mechanisms provided for doing so
	• designated individual(s) use organizational mechanisms to deploy the learning that is captured across the organization

the level. There are plenty of problems to solve and bugs to iron out — but eventually there comes a point where a move to the next level is required. At this point the organization needs to take a step back and reconfigure its approach to CI — and doing this involves learning of a different kind.

In both cases learning is not only about practising behaviours — it is also about finding ways of overcoming blockages at particular points. But learning isn't easy — and many organizations don't learn at all. Others get blocked at particular points and never move on from there — which goes a long way to explain why so many

CI programmes, despite early enthusiasm and commitment, eventually peter out.

WHY IT MATTERS

CI is important for any organization for at least three reasons:

- First, there is clear evidence of the value of sustained incremental change, chipping away at core problems of cost, time saving, quality improvement, etc. The 'lean revolution' owes much to harnessing this powerful engine for change.

- Second, even if we are working with radical innovation, utilizing breakthrough thinking it still takes a great deal of incremental improvement to make it work. Getting the bugs out of the system, fine tuning the new process, squeezing the design performance out in practice — all of these depend on sustained incremental improvement.

- And third there is a strong motivational element. Instead of asking people to work as cogs in a machine, a little like Charlie Chaplin in the film 'Modern Times', CI offers a way of empowering them. They can take some control over their working activities, use their knowledge and ideas to make a difference — and there is good psychological evidence of the value of doing so. An engaged workforce is a productive workforce.

WHY IT MATTERS TO HELLA

CI isn't new to Hella; it was a critical part of the strategy during the 1990s which underpinned so much of today's success. The 'Lopez era' in the automobile industry brought with it a survival imperative — either reduce costs, improve quality and cut delivery time, or leave the business. As Dr. Behrend pointed out, for Hella it was a simple question — '*to be or not to be*!'

Central to the company's way forward was finding ways to engage employees in the process of sustained incremental innovation. This wasn't just a new management technique but a fundamental shift in the underlying mental model which frames what the organization does — a 'paradigm innovation'.

The core value in such a culture — and one which has been with Hella from its earliest days — is 'entrepreneurial responsibility'. It's a two-way thing — from the employees there is the expectation that they will deliver their creativity and energy towards continuous improvement, and from the management side, that they will create the conditions within which people feel fulfilled, supported, given a sense of purpose and the opportunity to make their contribution.

A critical element in this is the idea of seeing employees as competent and responsible partners — and trusting them to behave as such. It needs leaders who are prepared not only to share these values but also to 'walk the talk', creating conditions in which there is reliability and trustworthiness, information and transparency, communication and creativity. And it particularly requires an attitude towards mistakes — innovation involves risks and experiments and these may not always work.

For Hella in the 1990s this was a challenge and an opportunity; as Dr. Behrend wrote in a report to the Board recommending CI:

> *If our employees are convinced that at HELLA these goals and guidelines can work together, then it is my belief that it will be a significant precondition for greater success for HELLA in the 90s. (12 March, 1991)*

CI was embodied in the Total Quality Management concept introduced in 1991, which built on three core principles:

1. Customer satisfaction as top target

2. Employees to be empowered and able to guarantee customer satisfaction

3. Entrepreneurial responsibility — the strategic guideline for processes and organizational structures to support this

It worked — and one measure of success was that it helped Hella
survive and grow.

WHAT HELLA IS CURRENTLY DOING

In today's environment CI is just as relevant, perhaps more so. It
is still an active part of Hella's innovation strategy but there has
been a drift away from a focus on quality, time and cost improvements towards one where cost seems to be the only important
factor. So there is strong interest in relaunching CI across the
company, trying again to build high involvement innovation. The
vision is one in which CI again becomes an intrinsic way of working at Hella — a strategic enabler.

To move this forward the company carried out a strategic
review which highlighted a number of challenges, including:

- refocusing CI back on the wider set of improvement objectives
  with which it had begun in the 1990s. Increasingly, CI was
  being seen as equivalent to cost-reduction and some of the other
  potential contributions (e.g. time saving) the approach could
  make were being marginalized

- moving from a project to a process base. Early CI efforts were
  around focused and targeted programmes — some, like the
  LION initiative, were highly successful in helping turn the lighting division around. But there is also scope for extending the
  approach and for lining it to a wider approach of continuous
  process improvement

- realigning the culture to one which supports the core values of
  CI and links these to a disciplined process

- aligning strategy with CI — policy deployment of the kind described in the framework model earlier

The challenge here is less about learning new routines for innovation management than in adapting and extending them, fine-tuning their implementation and spreading them to new application areas.

FURTHER RESOURCES

You can find a number of useful resources — case studies, video and audio, and tools to explore some of the themes discussed in this chapter at www.innovation-portal.info

In particular:

- Case studies of CI and its implementation in several organizations — NPI, Hosiden, Forte, Kumba Resources

- Video interviews with managers responsible for CI implementation in Veeder Root, Denso Systems, Redgate Software, Innocent Fruit Juices and the UK Met Office

- Various tools and techniques to help enable CI

- A framework model and assessment tool for exploring CI capability/maturity within organizations

REFLECTION QUESTIONS

1. Imagine it is 2020 and you are on a visit to Hella. What has the company done to ensure the CI culture it wants? What's happening around the place. What can you see, hear, measure? How has CI become 'the way we do things around here?'

2. You've been asked as consultant to a large organization to help them develop a culture of continuous improvement. What

would you recommend and how would you frame their next steps in terms of building in the structures and behaviours they will need for CI?

3. Use the framework tool on the Innovation Portal (high involvement innovation assessment) to identify where and how an organization of your choice might develop its CI capability.

NOTES

1. See Juran (1985).

2. For more background on the emergence of CI see Boer et al. (1999), Bessant (2003) and Schroeder and Robinson (2004).

3. There is a detailed analysis of the challenge in implementing quality circles in Lillrank and Kano (1990).

4. See, for example, Schonberger (1982).

5. In particular, the idea of 'lean manufacturing' captured this model — see, for more details, Womack and Jones (2005).

6. See Deming (1986).

7. For details of the research see Bessant, Caffyn and Gallagher (2001).

8

FRUGAL INNOVATION

Say the word 'frugal' and it conjures images of making do, eking out scarce resources, managing on a shoestring. And in the world of innovation there are plenty of examples where this principle has triggered interesting solutions. For example, Alfredo Moser's idea of re-using Coke bottles as domestic lighting in the favelas of Rio has led to its use in around a million homes around the world.[1] And potter Mansukhbhai Prajapati's Mitticool ceramic refrigerator offers a low cost way of keeping food cold without the need for power.[2]

'Frugal innovation' is a phrase which is becoming increasingly visible — for example, *The Economist* devoted a Special Issue to it and there are several management conferences exploring this theme. 'Frugal' means 'careful with resources' and in the business world it is increasingly used to describe an approach to innovation which is simple and sustainable. It grew out of experiences in locations where shortages of key resources required ingenious solutions to problems and where the simplicity of such innovations permits their widespread diffusion.[3]

But frugal is not simply about low cost improvized solutions in a resource constrained part of the world.[4] It's a mindset with powerful implications for even the most advanced organization. Sometimes, crisis conditions and resource scarcity trigger search in new directions, leading to radical and unexpected alternatives.

The underlying ideas of frugal innovation are to simplify products and services to the point where they are 'good enough' to meet widespread needs but not wasteful in terms of excess or unnecessary functions. It's an approach that has become important in meeting the needs of the emerging world where large populations represent significant markets but where individual purchasing power is limited. The management researcher C.K. Prahalad wrote persuasively about this in his 2005 book 'The fortune at the bottom of the pyramid', arguing that whilst several billion people lived on incomes of less than $2/day this did not mean they did not share needs and desires for goods and services, only that the ways those were designed and delivered would need to change.[5]

This challenge to innovation has become increasingly visible and important in many sectors, from consumer goods through to cars, telecommunications and healthcare. Different labels have been used — for example, 'jugaad innovation' refers to a Hindi word meaning improvization and flexibility to solve an urgent problem.[6]

For example, when Indian eye surgeon Dr Govindappa Venkataswamy retired he wanted to bring safe reliable cataract surgery to the poor in the villages of his home state of Tamil Nadu. The context was not favourable — even by Indian standards the cost of the operation (around $300) put it beyond the reach of millions living close to the poverty line, and there were additional constraints around the availability of skilled staff to carry out the procedure. Undeterred he searched for alternative approaches which could bring the cost down to around $30 — and he found an answer in a surprizing place, underneath McDonald's golden arches. His argument was that the same techniques used for fast food production and service (which relied largely on unskilled labour narrowly trained up in key areas) could apply in eye surgery. His Aravind Clinic was founded in 1976; today, it treats upwards of a quarter of a million people every year and has the distinction of having given back sight to over 12 million people around the world who would otherwise have gone blind because they couldn't afford the operation.[7]

What began as a 'frugal' innovation has grown into a global system offering some of the best eye care in the world. It has spawned multiple innovations — in education, preventive care and in replacing expensive replacement lenses with a much cheaper alternative designed for the Indian context (Aurolab is now the world's largest producer, exporting to 87 countries).

This new 'platform' model of reliable, low cost but safe healthcare has been taken up by others. Devi Shetty, once heart surgeon to Mother Teresa, has been christened the 'Henry Ford of heart surgery' for his application of it to complex operations like by-pass surgery. As with Aravind the massive savings in time and cost are not at the expense of quality; his Narayana Hospitals boast quality rates better than many western hospitals. And like Aravind emphasis is on a *systems* approach often challenging conventional business models for healthcare; for example, 12 million farmers now pay a monthly micro-insurance premium of 12 cents to receive widespread healthcare benefits. Using advanced telemedicine means that problems of skill shortages and expert coverage across a vast subcontinent can be dealt with using sophisticated IT infrastructure.[8]

Others are imitating this approach — for example, in China, software giant Neusoft are pioneering the use of advanced telemedicine to help deal with the growing crisis in which 0.5 billion people will need healthcare. Instead of building more hospitals the plan is to develop an advanced IT-supported infrastructure to offer a network of primary care — a 'virtual hospital' model at much lower cost and with much wider outreach.

WHY FRUGAL MATTERS IN THE INNOVATION WORLD

Stories like this abound and suggest that frugal approaches represent a rich opportunity for working in emerging markets. Frugal innovation offers new possibilities for a multinational player working in global markets to improve its performance in those areas with low-income high volume market characteristics. That has certainly been the case with consumer goods, and companies like P&G and Unilever have built strong businesses on the back of this model.

But it would be too easy to dismiss frugal innovation as only being about simple products and services for low wage economies; in fact, there are some powerful lessons and messages of relevance to a large and advanced organization like Hella.

In particular, there is a strong argument that sees frugal innovation as a forced shift in innovation trajectory. Where resources are scarce — for example, limited in physical or financial terms — then mainstream solutions become unavailable. Instead, problems need to be solved in different fashion — often leading to very different approaches. This is a powerful source of radical innovation because researchers looking for solutions are forced to go 'off road' rather than follow a main highway.[9]

We've seen this in the past — the origins of 'lean thinking' go back to the severe resource constraints experienced in post-war Japanese factories. Faced with shortages of materials, equipment, skills, they had no option but to develop an alternative approach based on minimizing waste. It didn't happen overnight but the constant attack on waste led to a powerful new model, one which has implications for process innovation around the world in both manufacturing and service sectors.[10]

And if the market opportunities and the potential for shifting innovation trajectory are not sufficient reasons to explore frugal, there is a third — the potential threat of disruption and the challenges posed by 'reverse innovation'. Whilst frugal innovation is associated with emerging market conditions where purchasing power is low, there is also potential for such ideas to transfer back to industrialized markets. GE's simple ECG machine (the MAC 400) was originally developed for use in rural India but has become widely successful in other markets because of its simplicity and low cost. It was developed in 18 months for a 60% lower product cost, yet offers most of the key functions needed by healthcare professionals.

Siemens took a similar approach with its Somatom Spirit, designed in China as a low cost computer body scanner (CAT) machine. The target was to be affordable, easy to maintain, usable by low skilled staff; the resulting product costs 10% of a full-scale machine, increases throughput of patients by 30%, delivers 60% less radiation. Over half of production is now sold in international markets. In particular, Siemens took a 'SMART' approach based on key principles — simple (concentrating on the most important and widely used functions rather than going for the full state of the art), maintainable, affordable, reliable, (fast) time to market.[11]

Rajan Tata pioneered a frugal approach in developing the 'Nano' — essentially a safe, reliable car for the Indian mass market. The whole project, from component supply chain through to downstream repair and servicing was designed to a target price of $2,500. Early experience has been mixed but it has led others to move into the 'frugal' space, notably Renault-Nissan. Building on the success of a 'frugal' model (the Dacia/Logan platform in Europe) they established a design centre in Chennai to develop products for the local market. The Kwid SUV was launched in 2016 selling at $4,000 and has broken sales records with a healthy order book and despite strong competition.

NICE BUT NOT HERE ...?

It's easy to dismiss these examples as relevant only to a low-income emerging world — but there are several reasons why this would be a mistake. Frugal innovation is relevant because:

- Resources are increasingly scarce and organizations are looking for ways to do more with less. The frugal approach can be applied to intellectual and skilled resources as much as to physical ones — something of relevance in a world where R&D productivity is increasingly an issue. For example, the Indian Mangalaayan Mars orbiter spacecraft was successfully launched in 2013 at the first attempt. Despite the complexity of such a project this was developed three times faster than international rivals and for a tenth of their costs. Its success is attributed to frugal principles — simplifying the payload, re-using proven components and technology, etc.

- Crisis conditions can often force new thinking — something which research on creativity has highlighted. So the improvizational entrepreneurial skills of frugal innovators — nicely captured in the Hindi word 'jugaad' — could be an important tool to enable 'out of the box' thinking

- Frugal innovations have a habit of migrating from their original context to other locations where they offer better value. Think about low cost airlines — the model there was essentially one which stripped away all but the essential function of safe travel between two points. Originally targeted at travellers unable to afford mainstream offerings the model quickly disrupted the entire industry.

FRUGAL INNOVATION AS A MINDSET

There's clearly a lot going on and, importantly, some core principles emerging around a different way of thinking where innovation needs to be careful with resources. In particular:

- It's not a new discovery, — the idea has been around a long time in different forms

- It's not simply about cost cutting — it's about creating value with careful use of available resources, doing more with less

- It's not just about low tech solutions — it's about appropriate solutions and can involve clever applications of high-tech ideas

- It's not just about product innovation — it covers processes (e.g. Aravind), services (e.g. telemedicine, low cost airlines), etc.

- It's not just about the poor, finding solutions to meet the needs of the 'base of the pyramid' (BoP) with low incomes and scarce resources — it has wider application and implications. Although the BoP market is huge and growing, and a significant opportunity in itself, frugal solutions also offer alternatives in existing high value markets. The idea of 'reverse innovation' might also lead to disruption in those mainstream markets

- It's not just about China and India — there are examples of frugal approaches all around the world

- It's not a new management technique — it's a *philosophy*, born out of situations where resources need to be conserved, where creativity can help find new and appropriate solutions. That Hindi term — jugaad — essentially describes what good entrepreneurs do.

HOW TO MAKE IT HAPPEN?

So how might an organization begin to think about frugal innovation? There are some core principles which help make up the mindset:

- Simplify — not dumbing down but distilling the key necessary functions

- Focus on value — avoid overshoot, avoid waste

- Don't reinvent the wheel — adopt, adapt, re-use, recombine ideas from elsewhere

- Think horizontally — open up the innovation process, engage more minds on the job

- Platform thinking — build a simple frugal core and then add modules

- Continuous improvement — evolve and learn, best is the enemy of better

And for each of these there is a growing and robust toolkit to help develop methodologies around working in frugal fashion.

WHY IS THIS IMPORTANT FOR HELLA?

There are several answers to this, in particular:

- Like any large organization Hella faces challenges in the resource world. This is not simply a question of sustainability or continuing the lean journey they began 20 years ago. Strong business pressures, especially from key customers, force a continuing battle to reduce costs, reduce development times, etc.

- There are also societal pressures towards making better use of limited resources — and these are not just important for Hella's image but also as part of its core values

- Frugal makes good business sense — evidence is that there are both operational benefits but also strategic ones coming from the approach

- Given that most growth in the future is likely to come from emerging markets, exploration of frugal solutions that work in those contexts, could represent a major business opportunity. Early experience in India and China (including participating in the supply chains for Tata's Nano project) gives Hella a seat at what may prove to be an important table

- Hella already has local presence in India and China, and is well placed to learn about these approaches in tandem with its dominant approach to R&D and production

- Frugal appears to offer significant opportunities to enhance R&D productivity through reverse innovation, open innovation, recombinant innovation, etc. — as major players like GE and Siemens have discovered

- Investigating it further offers a degree of 'insurance' against being disrupted by low cost, good enough quality competitors. The comparison with the disruption in the airline industry from low cost players is worth making

There is already experience around the company — for example, work on the Nano in India where the price point for suppliers was a massive challenge. And the work on platform engineering — see Chapter 9 — gives some other impetus to the core principle. Similarly, 'agile' engineering is trying to take a lean approach to development — see Chapter 13.

CHALLENGES FOR HELLA

Frugal innovation works — but it comes with a challenge. 'How to do more with less' is at the heart of lean thinking and a hard principle to argue with. Except when it challenges some underlying core beliefs in an organization — and there is a risk that it might do just that in a company like Hella. One of the strengths of post-war German industry has been the emphasis on technical excellence backed up by rigorous attention to quality and detail. Not for nothing does Audi use this image to great effect in the United Kingdom with its advertising campaign — '*Vorsprung durch technik*'. This isn't just a statement about cars which embeds the idea of 'progress through technology' — it carries the whole story of German engineering as something reliable, technology led, quality assured.

Frugal challenges that — it's a way of thinking, which is all about solutions not being perfect but 'good enough' (and then a methodology of continuous improvement to make them better). It's about working with limited resources and configuring a solution — and then improving on it. A bottom-up rather than a top-down process. Value engineering for firms like Audi or Hella is typically about systematic application of algorithms designed to retain the core function but then to strip out costs — a top-down process of subtraction. Like cutting a block of metal to the required precision and form. But in frugal innovation it's the reverse — it's assembling and then adding on. Build a very simple basic platform — and then add to it.

Both models can work — but they don't necessarily meet in the same place. Bottom-up forces a very different trajectory, one based on learning and improving through short experimental cycles, and doing so in a context in which any solution is better than nothing (significantly this idea of working with unserved markets and co-evolving with them novel innovation solutions is at the heart of Christensen's theory of disruptive innovation).[12] If you start from a very low, 'good enough' simple base you will not be able to offer all the functionality of the high-tech solution. But through a process of learning in and with your market you will approach closer and closer to what it wants and from a lower cost base.

And understanding the frugal model helps with developing a platform approach that allows growth through adding modules to suit a diverse market. The case of airlines like Easyjet and Ryanair is instructive; they began like other low cost airlines to find solutions to the core problem of cutting away anything that didn't add the core value of what they were trying to do. Essentially, applying lean thinking using key principles of value analysis, value stream mapping and continuous improvement.

But, having fought their way to a simple frugal model, they are then free to add features and additional functionality back in. Their profitability comes from the optional extras they can offer; it can configure around a segmented market by building on its core platform.

Frugal opens up this 'platform-plus' option — but to get to the starting point requires letting go of an older model. For entrepreneurs this is easy because there is no alternative — Aravind and NHL are new models started from scratch with different principles. But doing so inside an established tradition is a problem because of the potential for a clash of values — adopting a 'good enough'/fast learning model as opposed to a high quality technical excellence first time approach.

For a company like Hella, with its strong commitment to R&D and an image of innovation leadership, there might be apparent risks in being seen as a 'frugal' player. But the approach is not incompatible with high technology or R&D intensity. For example, the Mangalayaan spacecraft is not a simple piece of technology — but its development built on core frugal principles like platform thinking, modularity, agile development and fast learning, etc. These are themes already being explored elsewhere within Hella.

SO WHAT IS HELLA DOING?

Most importantly, they are exploring the idea and not simply as a new management fashion. It is becoming increasingly clear that understanding and working with this mindset could be a powerful and possibly disruptive source of innovation. Not for nothing are chief executives like Jacques Immelt at GE and Carlos Ghosn of Nissan-Renault actively promoting the concept and the growing experience of organizations as diverse as Siemens, Unilever and Tata underlines its potential. It is not incompatible with some of the core approaches already espoused by Hella — for example, the idea of using platforms to make better use of expensive knowledge resources. Given the large commitment of the company in emerging markets like India and China, it also makes sense to explore the potential for bottom-up innovation to come from there.

In terms of more specific actions the concept has a champion in the person of Naveen Gautem, an Executive Board Member within the electronics division who is passionate about it. He is already looking for ways to capture the Indian experience and transfer this elsewhere in Hella thinking, and it was he who led an i-Circle discussion of the concept during 2016. Since then he has been promoting some radical ideas to take this further within the company.

Part of this involves working in India and using frugal solutions and perspectives to help meet challenges in the local context. Hella's experience with supplying parts for the Tata Nano offers a good example of the continuing learning going on around frugal techniques and this is being concentrated in the Hella Technical Centre in Pune.

FURTHER RESOURCES

You can find a number of useful resources — case studies, video and audio, and tools to explore some of the themes discussed in this chapter at www.innovation-portal.info

In particular:

Case studies of organizations exploring frugal approaches including Aravind Eye Care, NHL Hospitals, Lifespring Hospitals.

REFLECTION QUESTIONS

1. Is frugal innovation simply a solution for low income developing countries — or could the principles be applied in any organization?

2. What are the barriers that might prevent this approach being adopted?

3. Can you find and explore examples of its effective application in advanced industrialized countries?

4. Are there opportunities for 'reverse innovation' and could they be a source of disruptive innovation?

5. If you were a consultant asked to report to the Board of Hella (or another major international company) about frugal innovation what advice would you give, and why?

NOTES

1. See http://www.bbc.co.uk/news/magazine-23536914

2. See http://www.thebetterindia.com/14711/mitticool-rural-innovation-nif-mansukhbhai/

3. For example, the problem in many shanty towns and temporary settlements is how to provide light when there is rarely any electric power available, and, even if there were, people are not able to afford it. By the simple use of an old plastic bottle with some liquid inside (containing bleach to keep the bottle clean) a window can be made in the roof through which light can pass. Alfredo Moser, a Brazilian mechanic, is credited with this idea which has diffused widely; over a million homes in Brazil now make use of this idea. http://www.bbc.com/news/magazine-23536914

4. There's an excellent website and network on the topic here http://frugalinnovationhub.com/en/

5. Prahalad (2006).

6. Navi Radjou gives a good TED talk on the approach: http://www.ted.com/talks/navi_radjou_creative_problem_solving_in_the_face_of_extreme_limits?language=en

7. http://www.innovation-portal.info/resources/aravind-eye-clinics/

8. http://www.innovation-portal.info/resources/narayana-hrudayalaya-hospitals-nhl-2/

9. Gibbert, Hoegl, and Valikangas (2007), Goller and Bessant (2017).

10. Womack and Jones (1996).

11. More details at http://www.nesta.org.uk/sites/default/files/our_
frugal_future.pdf

12. Christensen (1997).

9

PLATFORM THINKING FOR INNOVATION

Watch any group of kids playing with Lego and you'll quickly get the idea behind platform thinking. A small number of standard modular components linked to a basic architecture — and you can build almost anything! Close your eyes and very soon you'll be enjoying yourself remembering playing with those coloured bricks, wheels and other components. And whilst you may have bought a particular model most of the pleasure comes from re-assembly into new and unplanned designs. Millions of homes have the Lego box into which children (and not a few adults as well!) dive to let their imaginations run riot. And a visit to Legoland gives you part of the same experience on a large scale. Never mind if it's pouring with rain, just go into a large hall, dig into the huge mountains of Lego and create ….

Now think about your smart phone — what you're holding in your hand is a platform device with a basic architecture to which you can add the range of apps that you particularly want to make it work for you. This is mass customization, each phone giving the user what they want but made economically possible by platform thinking.

Although there's a buzz about the word now, platforms have actually been around a long time. Back in the 1920s Harry Ferguson developed a device to put on the back of tractors which enabled farmers to hook up all sorts of tools and equipment. The business model was simple — buy the basic tractor and add on the tools you want. Ken Wood's idea for domestic kitchen equipment followed the same pattern and it was one which Black and Decker and other power tool makers took to the DIY market. And IBM opened up the personal computer business by coming up with a platform architecture around which thousands of hardware and software developers could work.

The model goes deep inside the workings of product architecture. Intel's breakthrough into becoming 'Intel inside' at the heart of so many devices came from switching from discrete products to platform architectures, and consciously working to develop that mode of thinking across all of its design.

Of course it's not just products — services too benefit from a platform approach. eBay's model for online auctions paved the way for a wide range of enabling platforms for services — ride sharing (BlaBlaCar), accommodation (AirBnB) and mobility solutions (Über).

And, increasingly, the value of data as platform knowledge is becoming clear — for example, Nokia recently sold its Here geographical information business for $2bn to a consortium of European car makers. The UK's Ordnance Survey is a government agency that sits on a similar treasure trove of knowledge, which it currently deploys in the form of maps to help walkers find their way across the beautiful countryside. But they're also working hard to explore new ways in which they can deploy their knowledge base more effectively.

In an IoT (internet of things) world there's huge potential for capturing data from multiple devices and using it to create a platform across which different goods and services can be offered. That's why Amazon, Cisco and IBM have been busy investing in the backbone technologies, and where receptionists like Alexa, Siri and the voice behind Google's Home might soon be sitting at the entrance to a huge knowledge store.

Platforms have become high fashion — a recent Accenture report suggested that 81% of the executives they interviewed see them as central to their strategy over the next three years. And depending on how you define it the platform economy is valued at around \$2.6 trillion.[1]

The risk, of course, with something like this is that everybody jumps on the bandwagon and labels what they're doing as a platform. Just like Humpty Dumpty in Alice in Wonderland they use words — in this case the word 'platform' — to mean whatever it is they want them to mean! Perhaps a more helpful approach is to move away from the labelling of everything as a platform and look at the key elements in the thinking underpinning the approach.

WHY DO IT?

Platform thinking is just that — a way of thinking about your resource base and how to use it effectively. It might be embodied in physical products or services but at heart it's about knowledge and how you can offset the costs of learning something by deploying it widely in innovations that create value for different users.

Think of the Lego example again but imagine that the coloured bricks represent modules containing your key knowledge. The challenge then is not to build and sell a single design but to explore all the different ways in which you could configure them. And you could even take a leaf out of Lego's book and start to work with your users, co-creating new applications based on their ideas for using your bricks.

Platforms offer several routes to reusing hard-won knowledge — for example:

- Reusing expensive core product and process knowledge — as Black and Decker did, sharing the common drive and power for their tools across many variations on the theme. The idea of 'product families' is an old one but to make it work requires careful planning of both process (to create the flexibility in the system) and product (to design within these parameters).[2] The same thing is happening in services where the core knowledge to create the platform — for ride sharing, auctions or whatever — can be leveraged in different applications.

- Knowledge extension — stretching a design to cover the development costs through incremental building on the core model. For example, the Douglas DC3, originally introduced in 1935, sold over 10,000 units and is still flying today. It was knocked off its perch by the Boeing 737, still in production in new variants since its first flight in 1965. Back in the 1980s Roy Rothwell and others were talking about 'robust design' — essentially ways of spreading the core knowledge across as wide a field of application and for as long as possible.[3]

- Knowledge recombination — using the same core knowledge in different markets. For example, Procter and Gamble developed cyclodextrin chemistry as a way of handling odour masking by binding noxious molecules to its core structure. Originally deployed in Febreze as a spray, the technology had since found its way into scents, plug in oil diffusers, air fresheners and candles.

- Enabling a business model based on an architecture of core plus add-on modules allows many different market segments to be addressed. Easyjet's strength in the airline industry rests on having built an effective low-cost core platform and then adding (very profitable) services (like business lounges or priority seating) back in. Tesla has taken the concept further, building in many functions into all their cars, enabling them via software for those users requiring (and prepared to pay for) them.

- Accelerating adoption of innovation by allowing a free trial of core functionality and then allowing users to buy the additional features and functionality which they value — the 'freemium' model.

- Providing the keystone piece in a bigger puzzle. The Ferguson tractor system led to many people supplying the add-ons, creating a system model which, decades later, Intel were to use to advantage. As Annabelle Gawer and Michael Cusumano's work shows, 'Intel inside' is much more than a marketing slogan, it accurately describes a highly successful platform strategy.[4]

- Co-creating with users — allowing users access to your platform to create their own applications, amplifying your own offer and building new markets. Lego has been very successful at engaging user-designers and sharing their ideas and products with a wider market. Their Lego Ideas platform provides not only a valuable amplifier for their own designs but also valuable market and design intelligence about key trends.

- Building open communities in which the core platform becomes the basis for a linked ecosystem, quickly sharing new ideas and variants. For example, during the Haiti earthquake in 2010 a community quickly emerged which used a mobile phone platform on which they wrote apps for reuniting displaced families, providing real-time disaster and damage mapping and enabling urgent cash transfer to help victims access food and medicines.[5]

MAKING PLATFORMS HAPPEN

Of course there's a big gap between espousing the idea and making it happen. First, it's important to remember that one size doesn't fit all — there are many variants on the platform approach and it is important to be clear which version is appropriate.

Second, it's important to think about how the underlying knowledge architecture works — which people have what knowledge and how can they be effectively brought together to create new configurations? This may pose a big challenge to the functional silo model still prevalent in many businesses. As Rebecca Henderson and Kim Clark pointed out in a famous piece of research, there's a risk to relying too much on a particular architecture — you may find it difficult to reconfigure if the game changes.[6]

This isn't just business school theory — it directly maps on to how knowledge is organized in a company. What often happens is that the organization follows the functional structure of the product. If it were a camera company then one department would concentrate on the design of the lens and another on the body of the camera and it would make sense for them to interact because of the need to ensure a smooth fit of the one inside the other. As long as changes only take place in the components the architecture underpinning the knowledge works fine.

But when that architecture changes — for example, moving from mechanical to electronic control, or designing for a mobile camera which needs to fit on a headband — then problems can emerge. New groups need to bring their knowledge to bear while the old relationships may need to be set aside. Finding ways to modify or even redesign the architecture is key — and the importance of platforms lies in part in finding a suitably generic architecture around which such organization can be developed.

And third, comes the question of how open you are prepared to be on your platform. Just as open innovation is exploring new ways of linking up with external sources of knowledge and combining these in new forms, so platforms are increasingly opening up to allow co-creation, complementary modules and other forms of knowledge sharing and recombination. Linux is probably the best-known example of such open co-creation across a platform community but there are a growing number of others, as Eric von Hippel points out in his book 'Free innovation'.[7]

WHY DOES THIS MATTER FOR HELLA?

Hella makes things in high volumes — it takes years to agree on a product which then has a long life in production. Its history has been about developing close partnerships with key customer and through that they co-create the ideas behind the next generations of components for lights, body electronics, etc. But doing this isn't easy — not least because of the changing pressures in the market-place. These include:

- Faster technology cycles and the demand for more variety means that customers want more features and want them imple-mented faster. And all of this without compromising on safety or quality, and certainly not on price.

- Consumers increasingly expect high levels of electronic and technology features, as standard — so the old curve of fitting to high end and then moving downstream (think electric windows) is accelerating.

- Markets are becoming competitive and there is growing pressure from key customers to find strategic partners, able to supply variety and speed, and to eliminate other suppliers.

But for Hella the pressures are in the other direction — standardization would be perfect! So how to balance these increasing pressures and still remain competitive? How to balance innovation with standardization? How to move to 'mass customi-sation' — the Holy Grail of giving everyone what they want with-out carrying the cost penalty?

That's a big enough challenge but the real issue for Hella is how it leverages its knowledge base. Spending nearly 10% of reve-nue on R&D requires that the knowledge this buys is put to good use, ideally spread across as many products as possible. It implies the need for a strategic approach to product development, one which emphasizes the platform as a core philosophy.

This is, of course, something Hella already knows a great deal about — platform thinking is one of the core themes running through its innovation history. Right back to the Hella system in the early 20th Century the approach has been to gain leverage across different applications from a core platform knowledge base.

Whilst the principles are well known the challenge remains in implementing such a platform approach, especially based around integrating new technologies in hardware and software, mechanical and electronic design. This brings us back to the earlier discussion of architectural innovation and the challenge of knowledge organization and management. The key questions are around building a community and allowing members to share ideas and experiences; doing so requires not only a clear 'master' architecture for the platform but also organizations to change to ensure that issues of who talks to whom about what are clearly addressed.

How knowledge is arranged becomes important — and in an organization like Hella, where emphasis has been placed on creating specialist areas/functions with deep knowledge, the risk is that bridging between them may be difficult. Cross-functional working and process organization of knowledge flows becomes critical but this may challenge existing ways of working.

It is also critical to find ways of integrating customers into this community, bringing early warning of new direction around which to design while also shaping customer expectations around what is (or is not) possible with a platform plus modular architecture.

AND HOW IS HELLA RESPONDING TO THE CHALLENGE?

A good example of the way in which Hella is trying to bring forward its accumulated experience with platform thinking and link this with an increasingly customization-oriented strategy is in ongoing work around body control modules (BCMs).

A BCM is an increasingly important part of car electronics and essentially incorporates and works with many different functions — controlling windows, windscreen wipers, internal lighting, security, etc. It can have as many as 200 different inputs and outputs, and is part of the strong push to make the driver's space configurable to their particular needs and wishes. From a technical point of view this also means integrating many different signals flowing all around the car.

This is the direction in which car electronics has been moving for a long time — the problem comes with the rising costs of implementing all the different functionalities. When Hella offered its first electronic products back in the 1960s — simple indicator flashers — it was a very different world to today's multi-function and user configured situation.

Given our discussion above it's clear this is an opportunity to apply platform thinking to design and development. Is it possible to build a core platform architecture and then add modules to it configured to user needs? And maybe downstream even offer a two-sided platform in which third party 'apps' could be implemented across this?

Although Hella has been working with the concept of platforms for a long time, increasing market pressure to deliver increasing variety and customization has pushed the issue high in the innovation agenda.

THE JOURNEY TO PLATFORM THINKING

The problems with the current situation were identified back in early 2013 as being:

- Complexity of meeting different customer needs meant that development costs exceeding budgets

- Increasing pressure on time so development is increasingly in crisis mode

- No predictable base on which to build future strategy

To try and find a new way around these challenges, the company set up a Task Force in June 2013 for the BCM and its close cousin the 'Comfort Control Module' (CCM), concerned with various elements of in-car passenger experience like climate control, seat adjustment, etc.) with the short-term target of improving the profit margin and then, for the longer term, to develop and apply the new approach elsewhere using platforms as the growth engine.

Targets within this strategic framework were to

- Provide predictable project cost

- Provide a stable baseline for quotations and for commercial opportunity management

- Reduce design and development costs in customer projects

- Reduce team size for those projects

- Bring a high level of maturity earlier in the development phase

From the outset it was clear this wasn't just a technical challenge; in particular it raised questions in several areas:

People

Bringing everyone on board and changing the working culture, drawing on the skills and experience across the whole organization. This was achieved through developing a new process with key elements including:

- Town hall meeting

- Regular newsletter

- War room for keeping focus on the project
- Culture change training
- Overseen by a Change Control Board
- Convincing by performance and reinforcing the new way of working

Business

- Meeting the challenge of increasingly sophisticated and complex demands but competing against a small pool of suppliers
- Challenge of increasing order intake and achieving 'preferred supplier' status
- Building a competitive cost position
- Developing organizational excellence with a focus on KPIs
- Clear financial goals and business case for 2020 and beyond

Technology

- Developing a platform with both base system and modular features (the smartphone and apps model)
- Proof of concept and working prototypes
- Migration of concept into hardware
- Development of pathways to take OEM specifications and allow customization of features
- Concept of 'ownership' of platform features and base system
- Improvements and learning flow back through direct involvement of the platform team

Methodology

Changing the process from tool-driven development and then mapping methods to suit the tools into one which uses standard tools within a clear and systematic methodological framework.

REACHING THE DESTINATION?

At an i-Circle event in 2016 the team shared some of the successful achievements of the programme including:

- The profitability target was achieved
- Wide acceptance of the BCM/CCM Platform and potential to use it to acquire new business
- Worldwide rollout of the Platform
- Achievement of strategic supplier status for GM for Trailer Tow Modules

Building on this success there is now extensive effort across Hella to promote further platform applications.

FURTHER RESOURCES

You can find a number of useful resources — case studies, video and audio, and tools to explore some of the themes discussed in this chapter at www.innovation-portal.info

In particular:

- Case studies of organizations like Lego, Procter and Gamble, and Marshalls, which leverage their knowledge base in multiple applications through platform thinking

- Case examples of 'recombinant innovation' in which the same core elements can be redeployed in other fields — for example, Aravind eye clinics, 3M, Kodak, Fujifilm

- Tools to help explore themes raised in the chapter

REFLECTION QUESTIONS

1. Innovations can be 'architectural' — changes in the ways different things are put together into a whole system. And they can also be at the 'component' level — the parts which go into those systems. Looking at a sector of your choice, identify which of the changes happening over time are architectural and which are component. What are the implications for different players in terms of the likely threat to them and the ways in which they could respond?

2. Identify examples of platform innovation in organizations with which you are familiar. How does the underlying architecture support the reuse/recombination of knowledge investments over time?

3. You've been appointed as a consultant to a large organization looking to develop a platform strategy for its product and services. How would you advise them to proceed to maximize their significant investments in R&D and knowledge creation?

NOTES

1. https://www.accenture.com/gb-en/insight-digital-platform-economy

2. Gawer and Cusumano (2002).

3. http://onlinelibrary.wiley.com/doi/10.1111/j.1467-9310.1989.tb00635.x/abstract

4. Gawer and Cusumano (2002).

5. https://www.ted.com/talks/paul_conneally_digital_humanitarianism

6. Henderson and Clark (1990).

7. Von Hippel (2016).

10

OPENING UP INNOVATION NETWORKS

Walker's Wagon Wheel tavern in the late 1970s was a particularly important place in innovation. Its name provides a great description of its role — like spokes on a wheel people and ideas converged on its centre and on a Friday night the air was full of conversation. Ideas flew around the place, colliding and often crashing in flames on the floor. But some of them fused, became something bigger, began conversations which carried on over the coming weeks and grew into new businesses. Its location was also important — Mountain View, San Francisco, close to the emerging technology cluster of start-ups and big electronics firms, the sprawling campus of Stanford University ... Silicon Valley as it was to become.

Of course Silicon Valley today is different — not least because of the shift in the industrial and technological base. Whereas the 1970s were about the exploding new world of possibilities around microelectronics, today the region is a crucible for new thinking about artificial intelligence, smart connected devices, the Internet of Things, Industry 4.0. And in particular it's about the emerging new thinking about *mobility* — not just cars, trucks and buses but a whole new industry involving new players mixing with the old, mechanical technologies meeting the virtual, software and hardware combining in ever more exotic variants.

The old Wagon Wheel bar has gone (closed in 2003) but the role it played is as important as ever. Innovation is about creating value from ideas — and in the early stages when a new industry is emerging those ideas are widely distributed. It's critically important to have conversations, explore possibilities, make connections between different worlds of knowledge — *networking* is the name of the game.

DIFFERENT TIMES, DIFFERENT NETWORKS

When an industry is well-established patterns of innovation follow well-worn paths and trajectories. And the kind of network which helps there is based on what sociologist Mark Granovetter called 'strong ties' — close relationships between key players which build up over time. These links involve high levels of trust between players and their willingness to share information and risk mean that they can build towards a jointly bright future.[1]

But when the game is changing, when new trends in technology and across markets mean that the old models are breaking down then the networking takes on a different pattern. In this world strong ties can sometimes get in the way — we keep on talking to our old friends and partners without realizing that the game needs new links, bridging between very different worlds. These are called 'weak ties' — and they are important when new industries emerge, as we are seeing with the transition from the 'auto industry' to something involving driverless cars, shifting ownership and usage patterns, big regulatory pressures — the emerging 'mobility industry'.

WHY IT MATTERS ...

This newly emerging industry isn't there yet and it is hard to predict winners and losers. It's a space characterized by what two US professors, William Abernathy and James Utterback, call the 'fluid phase' of innovation.[2] This model suggests that in the early days of a major new technology or the emergence of a new market there are lots of people playing around with the new possibilities. Entrepreneurs of all shapes and sizes, from crazy inventors to shrewd businessmen, see possibilities and try stuff out. The result is a soup of possibilities, bubbling away, getting hotter and hotter — the 'fluid' phase. At this stage no-one knows what's going to emerge, which ideas will be winners, what the market wants — because that's equally fluid. Only gradually do some big ideas begin to converge until one day a 'dominant design' crystallizes out — not necessarily the most exotic technology but the one which fits best with what people want and value and which is technically possible.

That's when the innovation game changes; many of the early entrepreneurs fail and an industry begins to form around the dominant new idea. Emphasis shifts from finding that dominant design to making it work — and in the process many of the entrepreneurs who entered the field begin to leave it. More important, by that stage the threat to established players in the old industry is at its strongest; unless they have been involved in exploring the fluid phase and its possibilities they may find themselves overwhelmed by the next wave of innovation.

So the challenge is around finding new ways to work with the fluid state. How to handle the 'weak ties' question — how to find new partners, build relationships with them and begin to develop stronger ties with the key players? Organizations need to:

- Be in there — it's not enough to be an observer from the sidelines, too much is happening too quickly so being as close to the action as possible matters

- Be in there early — things evolve quickly in the fluid phase and it's important to spot key trends early and help to amplify and work with them

- Be in there actively — it's not enough to be a passive bystander, organizations need to begin the process of finding, forming and developing new networks

What it's not about is simple shopping for ideas — the fluid state means that there is no clear pattern about the winning innovations will be. Instead it involves:

- learning, gathering new information

- experimenting — trying out early stage ideas in simple prototype forms, playing with possibilities

- exploring new business models — the dominant design is essentially about value and how it is captured and delivered. We don't know the dominant design in advance and so we need to experiment with multiple models — but we also need to do so systematically, building use cases and exploring stories of how the proposed innovation will create value in people's lives

- networking — the theory of knowledge suggests that this phase is when 'weak ties' matter

It's essentially a social process of learning and network building, which is why the 'Wagon Wheel' model is important — finding ways to meet and make connections which could develop the future.

FINDING, FORMING AND PERFORMING — THE CHALLENGE OF KNOWLEDGE NETWORKING

While discontinuous changes of this type have occurred throughout history, there is evidence that they are becoming more frequent and more severe. And the problem for established organizations looking out to a wave of potentially disruptive discontinuity is that they need some very different approaches to deal with it. They can't simply stick to the knitting — though in the short term they might survive because of what is sometimes called the 'sailing ship effect'.

In the early days of steamships they were perceived as a threat which spurred the sailing ship industry to improve its performance. Steamships were also at the early stage of their development, prone to blowing up and breaking down; sailing clippers remained competitive for an extended period of time. But inexorably the new industry around steamships got better and gradually overtook and eventually marginalized the sailing vessels.[3]

But to move into the new world requires new approaches — behaviour patterns — within the organization which are better suited to exploring an emerging and still uncertain environment. This is very much the skill set we associate with entrepreneurs — but these behaviour patterns don't necessarily sit well alongside those of established mainstream innovation. This problem is compounded by the fact that the old models work well and are deeply embedded in structures which reward and reinforce these. In the short term it is these relationships which matter in terms of earning the money needed to support exploration of something new.

One of the key areas in which this emerges is the inertia around established networks and relationships. Long-term and deep relationships are powerful positive resources for incremental innovation but they may be a barrier preventing organizations form accessing new networks needed under discontinuous conditions. As Roland Burt put it, *'the ties that bind may become the ties that blind'*.[4]

Creating new networks to support discontinuous innovation provides an important source of new insights, competencies and relationships for the firm as it attempts to make sense of the changes affecting its industry. But constructing them requires paying attention to at least three key areas — finding, forming and performing.[5]

Finding

Finding refers essentially to the breadth of search that is conducted. How easy is it to identify the right individuals or organizations with which you want to interact? Do you already know exactly who they are, or will you need to put considerable effort into locating the right actors? Finding is enabled by the scope and diversity of your operations and by your capacity to move beyond the traditional way of thinking in your industry.

It's not easy — there are many barriers which can prevent making connections, like:

- Geographical — potential partners may not be in the same place

- Cultural — they may come from a different culture with different rules and expectations, one which you are unfamiliar with and have no access to

- Sectoral — they may be in a different technological or business world and your paths may not normally cross

- Institutional — they may inhabit very different worlds — for example there are big gaps between the worlds of the public and private sector

Forming

Forming refers to the attitude of prospective partners towards you. How keen are they likely to be to work with you? Do you expect them to work hard to build the relationship themselves, or do you expect them to resist your overtures because of their different perspectives? Figure 10.1 sets up a simple matrix to identify some of the positions and strategies which might be involved in trying to form new relationships.

The bottom-left zone 1 represents the relatively straightforward challenge of creating new networks with potential partners that are both easy to find and happy to do business with you.

Zone 2 opens up the challenge of locating the appropriate individuals or organizations from among the many thousands of prospective partners. But once found they are still interested in

Figure 10.1. Four Generic Approaches to Network Building.

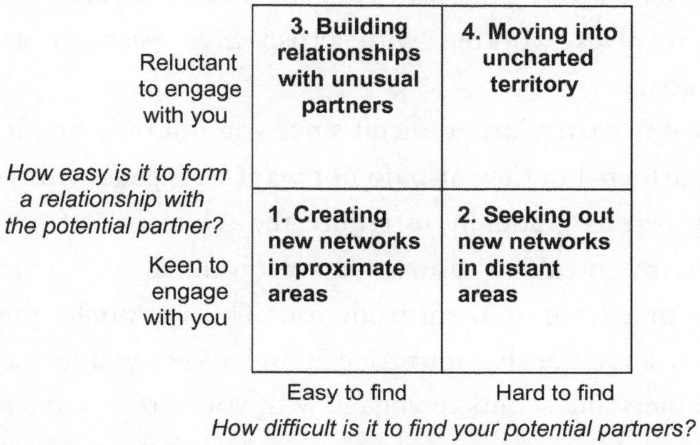

	Easy to find	Hard to find
Reluctant to engage with you	3. Building relationships with unusual partners	4. Moving into uncharted territory
Keen to engage with you	1. Creating new networks in proximate areas	2. Seeking out new networks in distant areas

How easy is it to form a relationship with the potential partner?

Easy to find   Hard to find

How difficult is it to find your potential partners?

developing a relationship with you. An effective strategy here is to use boundary-spanners and scouts who can forge links with potential partners. Boundary-spanners are individuals who understand both worlds and can make the necessary links between them. Scouts are individuals who have or are prepared to build diverse networks into places or sectors that your firm is unfamiliar with.

A good example is the long-standing investment which the UK communications company BT has made in Silicon Valley. This was always seen as a scouting operation and while the number of successful partnerships that result from this activity is small — typically four or five per year — the unit serves an invaluable role in keeping BT abreast of the latest developments in its technology domain. As Jean-Marc Frangos, the head of the unit observed,

> *The most important thing is to have your radar in such a way so the technologies you identify at Silicon Valley are really useful as opposed to 'a nice to have'. Being able to identify the mapping of what you see with the various interests is the challenge here .... You won't find the cure for your patient if you don't really understand what he suffers from.*

Zone 3 is where potential partners are easy to find but potentially reluctant to engage with you. An effective strategy in this situation involves working with prospective partners around a shared goal.

Zone 4 is particularly difficult since you not only find it hard to locate partners but they also do not want to engage with you. One strategy here is gradually to reduce the reluctance of prospective partners by breaking down the institutional or demographic barriers that separate them from you. This essentially pushes the prospective relationship into zone 2, and allows you to use boundary-spanners and scouts to engage with your prospective partners. It requires 'safe' spaces where open-ended conversations and exploration can take place — and we have seen considerable interest and growth in the provision for such innovation spaces and hubs to allow such conversations to happen.

Performing

The third challenge involves turning new networks into valuable and high-performing relationships with partners. Once again this requires overcoming several barriers such as different attitudes towards the protection of Intellectual Property, and development of trust and confidence to share risks.

Part of this process involves building networks in anticipation of future needs, rather than to tackle an immediate and pressing problem. For example, the international network of scientists P&G created as part of its Connect & Develop model is not on the company's payroll, and is not required to deliver any ongoing services to the company, but its *latent* value — its ability to spring into action when requested — is enormous. In such cases, the challenge is one of creating realistic expectations and ensuring that the members in the network are kept up to date with developments inside the company.

Network partnerships also rely on trust and reciprocity to be effective, and increasingly firms are realizing that the more they give away, the more they get back in return.

Networks are also different from other forms of strategic relationships in that the source of power may be spread across many players rather than concentrated. It is important to strike a balance between facilitating network connections and organizations seeing themselves as network 'orchestrators' who achieve some level of control by virtue of their central position in the network.

WHY DOES THIS MATTER TO HELLA?

We've already seen that the certainties around the automotive industry have begun to disappear and a combination of technological, market, social and regulatory forces are reshaping the environment. It is beginning to look like a very fluid space in which many new innovation possibilities are bubbling away — the challenge is how to find key players and engage with them early enough to build effective networks and relationships.

This is a particular challenge because Hella not only faces the need to construct new networks but also to review and possibly let go of some of its existing 'strong ties'.

SO WHAT IS HELLA DOING?

That's what Hella has been doing for the past year, working with a new group, Hella Ventures, based in the heart of Silicon Valley. Its role is to position the company to take advantage of the exciting new developments in the emerging mobility world. The underlying strategy is very similar to that of the UK telecoms firm BT, and involves building up a team of scouts and boundary-spanners to help connect Hella to the newly emerging world of opportunities.

The role of Hella Ventures is primarily one of making connections, often outside of Hella's 'normal' world but linking across to key players who may well be important to the company in the future. In the emerging new world of intelligent mobility Hella could be in a strong position, with its deep understanding of sensors and actuators — something which makes it attractive to others as a potential partner in emerging new ventures.

Why is Hella Ventures located in Silicon Valley? It's clear that there's a great deal of activity going on — the analyst firm CB Insights reported a 77% increase in ventures and deals around 'auto technology' in 2016 alone. And Hella wants to have a seat at the table as this game begins to play out. Hella Ventures is located in Sunnyvale, right in the centre of the Valley and close to major auto and electronic players. As Jason Waterman, MD of Hella Ventures pointed out at a recent i-Circle, proximity matters here — you can't just fly in and pick up on the many conversations and the flow of ideas, you need to be there.

At the heart of his presentation was a map, a network of connections which Hella is beginning to make and which may lead to interesting developments. Importantly these network partners are not just on the technology side; much of the conversation is about finding value propositions, use cases and business models which mobilize ideas like cloud based data and machine learning. Having a presence there has already meant that several senior Hella managers have been able to meet and explore with potential partners — for example visiting Toyota's huge Stanford-linked research centre. And Hella is actively trying to catalyze new links — for example by sponsoring conferences and workshops exploring the theme of disruptive technologies.

From a strategy point of view Hella is looking to identify and partner with interesting new ventures — the aim is to build networks to be able to spot 'diamonds in the rough' and make selective investments there. These would be earlier stage and lower level — the intention is not to swim in the 'red ocean' where there are already many competitors but instead to find 'blue ocean' space. To help build the platform the Hella model involves networking, trying to connect with the local start-up culture, playing across a wide field, building partnerships through a targeted deal flow process.

Throughout the process there is the need to connect back to Hella's core knowledge base and look for useful synergies, fields where Hella has experience, key technologies and the ability to help scale the ventures.

Although very much a new approach there are already some valuable lessons emerging for the company. In particular:

- Top management support is essential, especially now as the emphasis moves from setting up the operation to using it to build new business

- Communication will be key — making sure the rest of Hella understands what is happening and ensuring that the right connections across the company are made early and actively

- Learning new ways of working with new partners — essentially opening up Hella's approach and building from 'weak ties' to stronger partnerships

- Return on investment — this is a new area and in the 'fluid phase' of innovation it isn't easy to identify a short-term return, a winner product. Much of the investment is into learning and building capability, developing the potential for what could be a key element of Hella's future. (In the 1980s Hella took a similar bold step by moving early into the field of microelectronics, building a capability over time. The short-term payback from that investment wasn't necessarily clear but 30 years later it has proved an important strategy.)

FURTHER RESOURCES

You can find a number of useful resources — case studies, video and audio, and tools to explore some of the themes discussed in this chapter at www.innovation-portal.info

In particular:

- Case studies of organizations and their networking strategies — for example, Procter and Gamble, 3M, Nokia

- Tools to help you explore themes raised in the chapter

- Video explaining strategies used by organizations to help them manage the 'knowledge spaghetti' challenge of open and sometimes discontinuous innovation

REFLECTION QUESTIONS

1. Using the frameworks described in the chapter how might you develop a network-building strategy for an organization seeking to move into new business space?

2. Explore (with examples) the strengths and weaknesses of taking a more open approach. For example, open innovation spreads the net more widely to find ideas — but it also raises big problems around intellectual property protection.

3. 'The problem for small firms isn't that they're small — it's that they're isolated'. How might networking help deal with the challenges of being an innovative small firm and what advantages might this approach offer?

4. 'Many hands make light work' — or 'Too many cooks spoil the broth?' Using examples, show why networking may be a positive or negative element in enabling successful innovation.

NOTES

1. Granovetter (1973).

2. Abernathy and Utterback (1975).

3. Gilfillan (1935).

4. Burt (2005).

5. Birkinshaw, Bessant and Delbridge (2007).

11

DEALING WITH DISCONTINUITY

When Sally Windmuller started tinkering around with accessories there wasn't a car industry as such. Instead a series of inventions had begun to pave the way for one — but quite what it would look like no one knew. There wasn't a market in the traditional sense — only a handful of people were wealthy enough to buy the new vehicles, each of which was being hand built in customized fashion. A visit to the town of Lippstadt showed plenty of personal transportation, all of it the horse and cart variety in its various forms. Two-seaters, four-seaters, omnibuses, flatbed trucks — any kind of cart pulled by almost any kind of animal. But a motor car?

And there wasn't an organized industry with a network of suppliers bringing in the parts, which a few large assemblers could put together to build vehicles to a standard design, and in the volumes needed to make them economic to sell to everyone. That revolution was to take another 30 years and the hands of Henry Ford and his team to bring to the streets of Germany. Instead there were entrepreneurs like himself, seeing latent opportunity and trying to find ways to convert it into something real.

Of course, anyone with a time machine could have seen what was coming and the huge changes in the marketplace for transportation. Sally Windmuller's instincts were right — this became a huge industry and effectively disrupted the cosy world of players linked too tightly to the horse and carriage world. Some of them adapted and moved on with the new technology, others fell by the wayside.

It's not always about spotting opportunity — sometimes it's about not being able to change fast enough when something different appears on the horizon. New industries based on new technologies bring with them big challenges for established players. It's a familiar pattern — think about many sectors which dominated the 19th Century and how those industries rose and then fell away as technology created new markets and drew customers away from the old businesses.

Back in the 1850s there was a huge industry in the northern USA based on ice harvesting — flooding fields, cutting blocks of ice, insulating them and shipping them southwards where they were needed to preserve food. Thousands of people working to produce millions of tons of ice — and all washed away by the wave of technological change triggered by Herr Linde working in his Munich laboratory on the development of refrigeration.[1]

Or the world of lighting — transformed by Thomas Edison, Joseph Swann and others to one based on the new technology of electricity. Suppliers of oil and wicks, candles and even gas lamps lost out as the new opportunities in the electric lighting field began to emerge. Entrepreneurs like Fredrik and Gerard Philips set up Philips Metaalgloeilampfabriek N.V. in Eindhoven in 1891 to take advantage of the new wave, riding it successfully towards becoming one of the world's largest electrical/electronics companies a century later.

PATTERNS OF INNOVATION

Fortunately discontinuity doesn't happen all the time — there are long periods in between where there is relative stability and which favour the established order. It's a pattern sometimes called 'punctuated equilibrium' — and understanding it can provide important clues for innovation management, because different strategies are needed at different points in time.[2]

During the early stages of a new technology or a new set of market conditions there is a 'fluid' stage in which neither technology nor market is mature and where the picture is of many entrepreneurs experimenting with possibilities. Most of these fail but eventually one model — not necessarily the most technologically sophisticated but the one which fits best with the market context — emerges to become the 'dominant design'.[3]

Like a crystal in a super-saturated solution this provides the point from which the industry grows and in its consolidation and maturity phase innovation follows a trajectory of incremental improvement. James Bright documented the growth of the lighting industry and showed how following the breakthroughs on which Edison and others built the industry, the growth then rested on a continuous stream of improvements. And although there were occasional flurries around the edges — fluorescent lights, xenon and other discharge technologies, etc. — the industry stayed pretty placid until the emergence of LEDs in the late part of the 20th Century. Radical innovation was replaced by systematic incremental improvement, especially around the processes though which lights were made in the increasingly concentrated and large-scale industry.

DISRUPTION FROM THE EDGE

In this model industries become increasingly mainstream, exploiting the dominant design in a stable network with a few strong players and deep relationships amongst key suppliers and major customers. But at the edge of this orderly world there are entrepreneurs constantly searching for chinks in the wall, overlooked doorways which might offer opportunities to enter the game and disrupt it.

One way of doing this involves finding a group of people whose needs are not being met or are met poorly by existing technologies. Think about low cost airlines and the challenge here was around *who* was doing the flying. There was an established mainstream market using a dominant design — most airlines looked and behaved in the same way, offering similar services and prices to customers (or their companies) rich enough to afford this mode of travel as an alternative to slower rail or road options. But a few entrepreneurs began asking the question 'who doesn't fly yet — but might?'

This led them to focus on the unserved markets — for example students, backpacker travellers or pensioners on limited incomes. Offering them the chance to fly would require some radical re-thinking of the product offer, something with few frills but the opportunity of a safe flight for a low cost. Behind the scenes a great deal of process innovation would be needed to cut costs, speed up expensive turnaround times at airports, multi-skill staff to improve labour productivity and so on.

All of this experimentation and learning took place at the edge — it was of little concern to a mainstream club of airlines operating out of central airports and serving their established markets. But gradually the new entrants refined their model and its offer began to attract customers from the mainstream — the financial logic was hard to escape. Safe simple flying at a fraction of the 'normal' price was very attractive over most short-haul routes — and suddenly the stable world of air travel was disrupted. Many major airlines couldn't make the transition and those which did follow the new entrants were for some time at a disadvantage until they too could learn the new rules of the game and the tricks whereby it could be played.

Disruption of this kind was first identified by U.S. professor Clayton Christensen who developed a theory around it, drawing on many cases from a variety of sectors.[4] Common to all of them was the role of entrepreneurs working at the edge and suing a new combination of technology — often simpler and cheaper — to provide a 'good enough' solution to the unmet needs of a fringe market. That innovation is then improved by learning from and with the new market and it draws other customers away from the mainstream, fuelling the accelerating move towards full-scale disruption.

It may not always be simpler technology or lower price but the model of disruption is based on things happening at the edge of the current market focus and involves new networks of layers — customers, suppliers, and above all entrepreneurs.

One of the roles played by entrepreneurs (first identified by Joseph Schumpeter, the godfather of innovation thinking) is 'creative destruction' — looking to disrupt with a better idea which simultaneously replaces the existing one. Nowhere is this more visible than in business model innovation where entrepreneurs change the rules of the game by creating a new and better game. Business models are basically a formulation of how an idea can create value, a roadmap for innovation. Changing the business model may involve new technology or serving different markets but it can also involve re-arranging the existing pieces in a new way. George Eastman's contribution was not to invent the camera but to find a way of bringing it into the homes of everyone. Henry Ford did the same with the motorcar and Steve Jobs with computing devices. Recent examples like Über or AirBnB simply bring a new way of organizing existing resources like cars or accommodation but they have similar transformative power.

DISCONTINUITY AND DISRUPTION

So we need to recognize that discontinuity happens — we can't always predict it but it is out there. It may come from technology or market trends, it may be entrepreneur-led — but it is going to happen. Whether it disrupts an industry or a particular organization's operations depends on how well placed that organization is to anticipate and act to minimize the threat, open up the opportunity.

WHAT'S THE PROBLEM?

The trouble is that the very things which allow an organization to move from being a start-up entrepreneurial venture to a large established business can also limit its ability to search at the edge and react quickly. All organizations begin as small start-ups and exploit the advantages of entrepreneurial spirit — agility, risk-taking, being able to spot opportunities and being flexible in finding ways to exploit them. As they grow so repeating the innovation trick becomes a matter of building structures and processes to make things happen. Innovation becomes more organized and operates as a system.

Such innovation systems offer a powerful engine for delivering growth based on innovations within core areas, exploiting technical and market knowledge to advantage. But they also run the risk of becoming too focused on the current business and of losing the entrepreneurial capacity to explore at the edges of the current business, finding unlikely opportunities and connecting them back to the mainstream.

This tension — between 'exploit' and 'explore' — is well known and common to all organizations. Smart businesses recognize the need for a capacity to operate in both worlds — to develop what is called 'ambidexterity' in their innovation approach. (Ambidextrous people can work with equal facility using either hand whereas most people have a dominant hand which they use for most tasks). They seek to build on their core strengths in their mainstream innovation systems but also to build a capacity to explore in different ways, to recapture the 'venture spirit' which characterized their early foundation.[5]

INNOVATION AS A FRAMING PROBLEM

Just as human beings need to develop mental models to simplify the confusion which the rich stimuli in their environment offers them, established organizations make use of simplifying frames. They 'look' at the environment and take note of elements which they consider relevant — threats to watch out for, opportunities to take advantage of, competitors and collaborators, etc. Constructing such frames helps give the organization some stability but it also defines the space within which it will search for innovation possibility.

In practice these models often converge around a core theme — although organizations might differ they often share common models about how their world behaves. So most firms in a particular sector will adopt similar ways of framing — assuming certain 'rules of the game', following certain trajectories in common. And this shapes where and how they tend to search for opportunities — it emerges over time but once established becomes the 'box' within which further innovation takes place.

It's difficult to think and work outside this box because it is reinforced by the structures, processes and tools which the organization uses in its day to day work. The problem is also that such ways of working are linked to a complex web of other players in the organization's 'value network' — its key competitors, customers and suppliers — who reinforce further the dominant way of seeing the world.

Powerful though they are, such frames are only models of how individuals and organizations think the world works. It is possible to see things differently, take into account new elements, pay attention to different things and come up with alternative solutions. This is, of course, exactly what entrepreneurs do when they try to find opportunities — they look at the world differently and see opportunity in a different way of framing things. And sometimes their new way of looking at things becomes a widely accepted one — and their innovation changes the game.[6]

Rather like the drunk who has lost his keys on the way home and is desperately searching for them under the nearest lamp-post 'because there is more light there', firms have a natural tendency to search in spaces which they already know and understand. But we know that the weak early warning signals of the emergence of totally new possibilities — radically different technologies, new markets with radically different needs, changing public opinion or political context — won't happen under our particular lamp-post. Instead they are out there in the darkness — so we have to find new ways of searching in space we aren't familiar with.

How can this be done? By luck, sometimes — except that simply being in the right place at the right time doesn't always help. History suggests that even when the new possibility is presented to the firm on a plate its internal capacity to see and act on the possibilities is often lacking. For example, the famous 'not invented here' effect has been observed on many occasions where an otherwise well-established and successful innovative firm rejects a new opportunity which turns out to be of major significance.

A MAP OF INNOVATION SEARCH SPACE

As we saw in Chapter 1, organizations need to explore a variety of areas in their search for innovation opportunities. **Figure 11.1** shows this simple map again.

Zone 1 corresponds to the 'exploit' area we looked at earlier where we are working in familiar territory and looking to exploit the knowledge base which we already have. Zone 2 is about exploring but within the context of our existing frame, pushing the frontiers but in directions we are familiar with. Zones 3 and 4 bring in new elements and combinations and requires a different and more open approach to search. This is especially tricky where the different elements interact with each other to make a complex

Figure 11.1. Exploring Innovation Space.

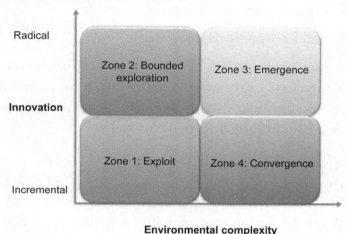

emergent system which is difficult to explore in systematic fashion.

Of course it isn't just about seeing what's around the corner — organizations also need to find ways of working with those threats/opportunities, creating new ventures and integrating them with their mainstream. Today's entrepreneurial experiment could be tomorrow's mainstream business.

The challenge for established organizations is that whilst they may have built effective systems for working in zones 1 and 2 they require very different capabilities to deal with the right hand side of the picture. In these areas the key skills are those of an entrepreneur, able to work flexible in unclear and fuzzy environments and experiment with possibilities in that space. The kind of characteristics needed here include:

● Flexibility — able to reframe, to see differently

● Explorer — open to new possibilities, challenge, adapt, change

● Agility — able to move amongst different options, link different worlds

- Ambiguity — tolerant of 'fuzzy' front end

- Risk-taking — prepared to experiment and fail

- Probe and learn approach to strategy

So mature organizations need two types of innovation structures, one focused on the mainstream and the other to manage the
very different challenge of exploring well beyond the lamp-post.

Table 11.1 illustrates these two 'archetypes'.

BUILDING INTERNAL ENTREPRENEURIAL CAPACITY

So how can an organization recapture a venture spirit and build
an entrepreneurial capacity? And once they've chosen a model
how can they make it work — what are the methods and tools to
enable innovation routines?

Many different approaches have been tried and we can usefully
position them along a spectrum of options, as in Figure 11.2.

The range runs from allowing people a little free time and the
license to think differently at one end through to setting up dedicated teams and structures and even spinning out a separate

Table 11.1. Two Different Types of Innovation Organization.

Type 1	Type 2
Clear and accepted set of rules of the game	No clear rules — these emerge over time. High tolerance for ambiguity
Strategies path dependent	Path-independent, emergent, probe and learn
Clear selection environment	Fuzzy, emergent selection environment
Selection and resource allocation linked to clear trajectories and criteria for fit	Risk taking, multiple parallel bets, tolerance of (fast) failure
Operating routines refined and stable	Operating patterns emergent and 'fuzzy'
Strong ties and knowledge flows along clear channels	Weak ties and peripheral vision important

Figure: 11.2. Options in Corporate Entrepreneurship.

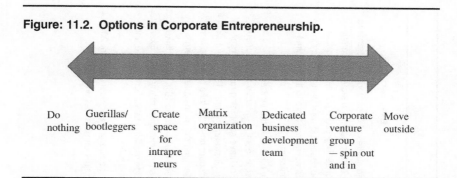

| Do nothing | Guerillas/ bootleggers | Create space for intrapre neurs | Matrix organization | Dedicated business development team | Corporate venture group — spin out and in | Move outside |

agency with the responsibility to act as an entrepreneurial satellite to the main business.

Each of these options has strengths and weaknesses and **Table 11.2** tries to summarize these.

The challenge to organizations is to configure from these choices a suitable response to the potential threat/opportunity in discontinuity. Rather than assume a single magic bullet most smart organizations seek a combination of responses drawing from across the spectrum. But increasingly there is interest in setting up a dedicated group to work apart from the mainstream business and operate in entrepreneurial fashion — a corporate venturing unit.

This sounds like a good idea — but it's important to recognize that these groups often fail to deliver on the (high) expectations of the parent organization. In particular research suggests that many failures can be attributed to wrong expectations — setting up vehicles without a clear understanding of what and how they can help. For many organizations the search is for new sources of growth but for others it is harvesting/exploiting what is there but underutilized. Julian Birkinshaw and colleagues carried out extensive research around this theme and identified four types of venturing:[7]

- *'Harvest' venturing* where the main aim is to turn underused resources into cash. A good example is Lucent ventures which

Table 11.2. Strengths and Weaknesses in Different Venturing Approaches.

Option	Strengths	Weaknesses	Examples
'Guerillas/bootleggers'. Most organizations will have some people who are 'natural' entrepreneurs and who may, from a mixture of frustration or enthusiasm, try to change things. They represent a potential source of innovation, especially if they can be identified and encouraged.	Natural motivation for change and the willingness to explore and take risks with new ideas.	Limited numbers and may find it difficult to operate in the corporate environment. Lack of time, resources and networking means they may end up frustrated and unable to achieve anything. In the worst case they may become so frustrated they leave and sometimes set up their new venture outside the business.	Some studies of frustrated entrepreneurs who end up having to leave the company because they could not get support; in some cases the new ventures they found are direct competitors to their original organization.

More positive is the incidence of 'intrapreneurs' — internal entrepreneurs who achieve something radical in spite of the mainstream system. They often work in their spare time and take pleasure from challenging the mainstream system. |
| Create space for intrapreneurs | Multiple minds looking at wide range of options — diversity and volume. | Limited resource commitment means that it may take a long time to create new venture. | 3M and their famous 15% policy, linked opt key successes over many years. Examples include masking tape, Scotch tape and Post-It notes. |
| Allow individuals some element of time and space within which they are encouraged to explore new ideas. | | Relies heavily on individual energy and effort to match the commitment by the organization. | Google allowing engineers to work 20% of their time on personal projects. |

This can be a long-term arrangement or a short-term campaign. For example many internal innovation contests (like 'Driving e-novation') are an attempt to mobilize such a venture spirit and to create the conditions within which people can surface novel ideas.	People will often bring their own energy and time to the projects on which they work.	Links to key people, resources, networks and knowledge may not be easily available in this 'bottom-up' approach.	Examples of innovations arising from this include Gmail. BMW encouraging 'bootleg' projects — they call them 'U-boot projects' which operate below the radar screen and are unofficially supported. The three series estate was developed by such a team in its early days. DeLaRue and their 'sabbatical' approach — also BAe Systems — encouraging new thinking and circulation. 'Driving e-novation'
Matrix organization allowing people a significant part of their time to play an entrepreneur role alongside their main role.	Allows more time and offers the potential to create mixed teams and combine knowledge sets.	Higher cost and formal resource commitment. Conflicts between core and entrepreneur roles. Bounded exploration because of time limits and pressures of the mainstream projects — sometimes hard for team members to reach 'escape velocity'	Temporary project teams working to create breakthrough thinking.
Dedicated entrepreneur development team	Full-time commitment and potential to create knowledge sets and networks.	Resource costs and tensions between the entrepreneurial group and the expectations of rest of organization.	Lockheed's 'Skunk works' where a dedicated team was licensed to think and operate outside the mainstream and which enabled breakthrough thinking around novel aircraft designs and stealth technology

Table 11.2. (*Continued*)

Option	Strengths	Weaknesses	Examples
	Can bring in outsiders to enhance diversity	Connections back to the mainstream may get lost and the team enjoy a different 'lifestyle' of which others are jealous and which separates them off.	Apple's 'pirate' team which developed the new i-computer
	Gives the group sufficient time, resources and a licence to search and explore	Problems of knowledge transfer and assimilation back into mainstream	BT's 'Wakaba' teams, dedicated short-term groups licensed to explore novel ideas
	Freedom and flexibility	Challenges of building a wider network of connections internally and externally beyond the team members	
	Small start-up culture	Risks and expectations sometimes out of alignment — short-term expectations for results	
		Problem of where to begin search beyond the lamp post and the difficulties of framing new ventures.	
Corporate venture groups — Spin out These are a full-time part of the organization with the responsibility to use	Offers ways of using the organizations' resources in novel fashion.	Costs of running a dedicated unit	University spin-off model — Silicon Valley, Route 128, Cambridge effect

the resources (knowledge, finance, systems, etc.) of the organization in novel ways and to open up new lines of business. They aim to spin out new ventures — as start-up businesses, as licences sold to others, as acquisition targets for others, etc. Intellectual property management	External focus, exploring new markets for knowledge and new business connections. Key part of an open innovation strategy	Risk of new ventures not succeeding Problems of finding new networks and connections	'Satellite ventures' — spin offs from the main organization but held in close orbit and often supported with key core services like HR, IT, etc.
Corporate venture groups — spin in. These mirror the above (and are often combined) but their focus is bringing in novel ideas from outside via licensing, merger/acquisition.	Acquire 'readymade' entrepreneurial culture and novel ideas	Finding relevant targets Assimilation problems — how to bring the knowledge into the mainstream Culture clash between old and new 'Elephant effect' where the rules, structures and operating procedures of the mainstream business stifle the entrepreneurial culture of the acquisition, like an elephant accidentally sitting on a mouse!	Pharmaceutical industry working with small biotech start-ups
Venture banking, where the group acts like a venture capital arm of the mainstream business, providing risk funds to support internal and external exploration			Corporate venture funding units in Intel, Nokia, etc. 3M internal venture bank

was set up to capitalize on the huge knowledge bank represented by Bell labs, essentially commercializing unwanted IP. It involves new venture start-up because existing routes to commercialize the IP like licensing don't work.

- *Eco-system venturing* where the company invests outside in key start-ups which may play a role in the wider ecosystem in which the parent company operates. An example would be Intel Ventures which looks for complementary businesses in its wide ecosystem and helps them get started. The value here is that they represent an extension of your knowledge base, a closely coupled network.

- *Venture capital venturing* where the company acts as a source of risk finance. This approach is difficult since venture banking is not the company's core expertise so unless there are particular skills or inside tracks there is a high probability of poor performance.

- *Innovation venturing* stimulating entrepreneurship within an existing function or area. The value here is that it creates entrepreneurial capacity to explore at the edges of the mainstream. Its advantages are around speed and breadth of search; a good example would be Shell's Gamechanger model which encourages extensive and future-based search for radical opportunities at the edge of the company's mainstream search space.

WHY IT MATTERS TO HELLA

As we saw in the introduction to this chapter Hella is facing a world which looks remarkably similar to the one in which Sally Windmuller began the business. Big technological changes which create opportunities for novel mobility solutions — think driverless cars, intelligence built into all aspects of mobility and suddenly we are in the realms of science fiction, like those images in 1960s movies. And equally big social and economic shifts which create very different market conditions — can we sustain the motor car as a model when it is playing a big role in choking our cities to death? Do we really need to own an expensive asset which spends most of its time lying idle — a status symbol which might have outlived its relevance for a younger generation? Is the option of integrated mobility the new Holy Grail and the solution no longer a car for Everyman but access to a reliable, cheap 24/7 transport option?

There's plenty of speculation in this world and equal parts of hype and hard evidence. But it certainly qualifies as a 'fluid state' in Abernathy and Utterback's terms and we can see — as they predicted — a swarm of entrepreneurial players exploring and experimenting in this space.

It's not just intelligent automobiles — the sustainability argument is also pushing the technological frontier with a similar fluid state around power systems. And this involves the network challenge just as Thomas Edison realized he needed a whole system of power generation and distribution to make his electric light bulb a commercial success so the electric or alternative fuel models like hydrogen need a network of support.

And it's not just technology there is a strong market element in this fluid state. Players like Tata and Renault-Nissan have placed heavy bets on the market growth coming from a new aspirational middle class wanting their version of the Model T promise — a car for Everyman which everyone can afford. The Nano, Kwid and other models are essentially the product of 'frugal engineering' simplifying down to a core low cost platform and then using scale economies to make this work and to then add back (at a premium) different modules.

And it's also about business models — there are opportunities in the space for rethinking the way the mobility game is played. Uber has grown from a small start-up to be the biggest provider of transportation services in the world — yet it doesn't own a single car or truck. Its business model around co-ordinated sharing across a platform represents another possible direction for innovation. Better Place was for a whilst the biggest start-up in history, able to attract over $200m in venture capital to get off the ground a novel model for solving the battery recharging problem with electric cars. It sounded plausible enough as a pitch to bring on board the ex-President of Israel and the Chief Executive of Renault-Nissan as active supporters and sponsors. It crashed spectacularly — but like any entrepreneurial idea in this fluid state it wasn't a complete failure, there were powerful lessons to be learned and other opportunities in the space.

So there's plenty going on and much of it has the potential to shake up a company like Hella. The challenge is to find ways of exploring a highly volatile space in which there are almost certainly powerful threats and rich opportunities. At the minimum there is a need for some insurance against being disrupted.

But Hella's innovation capacity is constrained. First of all it's very busy churning out an impressive stream of new products and the process technologies to support their delivery. There isn't the 'free' resource to explore at the edge.

Second Hella's networks are based on strong ties — they have been built up over decades and represent rich channels for information flow. But — as we saw in the previous chapter — there is a risk in this that the strong ties and well-developed value network is not necessarily the one which will matter in the future. And with architectural changes comes a risk of being cut off from the new important knowledge streams.

Third is the inertia common to any successful business — why swap a relatively low and manageable risk portfolio for oddball stuff with high risks and potential costs? How to encourage exploration when we're doing fine right now?

WHAT HELLA IS DOING

That's the rationale behind Hella Ventures, an initiative which the company has been taking during the past 3 years aimed at building capability to handle disruptive innovation. The origins of Hella Ventures go back to extensive discussions about the challenge of disruptive innovation and the need to develop a response; these were initiated by Jürgen Behrend and included workshops and an i-Circle meeting. This led to an internal 'white paper', a discussion document setting out the challenge and looking at two core questions:

- How should/could Hella approach the potential challenge of disruptive innovation — missing growth opportunities in a new wave? Or even being challenged at the heart of its core business?

- Which organization form — and accompanying tools, processes, techniques, governance, etc. — to adopt?

A range of possible strategies were explored and Hella Ventures emerged, with two main elements:

- A group based in Silicon Valley group looking to explore in the long-term (7 years plus) trying to pick up weak signals about key trends and lay the foundations for new networks to support entry into these emerging fields.

- A group based in Berlin group concentrating on a closer time-scale and looking to find leverage of Hella's knowledge base in new fields and to bring new technology/market opportunities to the relevant parts of the company.

The Silicon Valley operation (described in more detail in Chapter 10) is essentially a scouting operation whilst the Berlin group is an innovation venturing unit in the typology outlined earlier. Both groups were established in 2015 and have been on an extended learning journey with important lessons for both Hella's innovation capability and also its knowledge base.

An i-Circle meeting in early 2017 reviewed progress so far with the Berlin operation and members of the Hella ventures team shared some of the experience in developing not only a series of projects which may well have potential for Hella but also in creating an underlying capability for working with disruptive early-stage innovation ideas. They began by positioning the unit as a parallel effort going 'off-road' to explore possible new options for the company — as **Figure 11.3** suggests.

Working from new premises in an old electrical factory converted into start-up spaces the team (some 15 strong) have been working on a model of working based around entrepreneurial teams using an approach called 'lean start-up'. In essence this involves identifying possible areas of interest at the edge in terms of technologies and markets, and then quickly coming up with a 'minimum viable product' (MVP) which can be tested. The idea is not to design the perfect solution at the start but to start a learning journey — feedback quickly helps focus further development and

Figure 11.3. Exploring Disruptive Innovation.

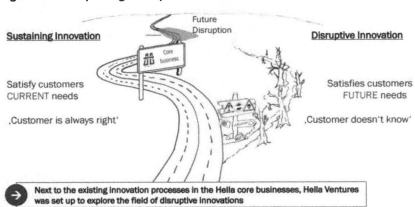

Figure 11.4. Fertile Ground for Disruptive Innovation.

Entrepreneurial teams to deliver proven concepts for potential new business

allows for 'pivoting' around the original ideas, strengthening it and sharpening the core concept (**Figure 11.4**).

Examples of such projects were presented, showing the fast learning and also highlighting some of the exciting new technologies with which the Berlin team are playing, including machine learning. They even brought a demonstration of a small robot vehicle which began to learn to find its way around a maze without hitting the walls.

RESULTS

It is still early in the life of Hella Ventures but there are already encouraging signs. First it is clear that a set of innovation routines have been developed and embedded; the ways of working around lean start-up and minimum viable product have become well-established and add to Hella's entrepreneurial skill-set. There have also been some early wins, with promising new ideas connected back to mainstream business units for further development.

The challenge for the future is to maintain the focus and develop a process for cycling through a stream of entrepreneurial ideas, building them into coherent business models and developing them to the point where they can be spun back into the company, spun out as standalone ventures or otherwise move forward.

FURTHER RESOURCES

You can find a number of useful resources — case studies, video and audio and tools to explore some of the themes discussed in this chapter at www.innovation-portal.info

In particular:

Case studies of sectors (imaging, music, lighting) and the patterns of change, continuous and discontinuous

Case studies of organizations and their approach to managing discontinuous change — Philips Lighting, Coloplast, Cerulean

Tools and frameworks for working with ideas raised in the chapter including a Discontinuous Innovation Audit

REFLECTION QUESTIONS

1. Find an example of a discontinuous shift — for example a major change in technology, markets or regulatory environment. Look at the players within that sector and explore what they did (or did not do) to ride with the waves of change. What else could they have done? Who were the newcomers trying to enter the space and how did they play their game?

2. You've been asked as consultants to recommend ways of enhancing innovation capability in a large organization similar to Hella. They already have effective 'steady state' capability for managing innovation under 'normal' conditions — what

else would you recommend? What structures and 'routines' do they need to:

— search beyond their lamp-post?

— handle the 'immune system' and persuade the company to do something very different?

— implement what may be alien ideas, incompatible with current skills, resources and 'how we do things here'?

3. What are the skills required to manage a unit set up to spearhead discontinuous innovation from within a large organization like Hella? How would you build a team to find and develop radical solutions whilst also maintaining the bridges back to the mainstream organization?

NOTES

1. Utterback (1994).

2. Tushman and Anderson (1987).

3. Abernathy and Utterback (1975).

4. Christensen (1997).

5. Birkinshaw and Gibson (2004) and Tushman and O'Reilly (1996).

6. Day and Schoemaker (2006).

7. Buckland, Hatcher, and Birkinshaw (2003).

12

AGILE INNOVATION

There's a paradox about innovation — it's all about change and yet the way we deliver that change needs to be part of a routine set of activities. Anyone might get lucky once but delivering a steady stream of innovations is going to need some form of structure, some repeatable process, some organization. As the noted management writer Peter Drucker pointed out, there is an underlying discipline to the act of innovation, particularly in the context of established organizations.[1] Start-ups might be able to get away with improvising and winging it but to survive and grow a mainstream business on innovation requires a lot more structure to the way we handle innovation.

And that's where the problems often start; how to balance the discipline and control over scarce resources with the creativity and inspiration which finding a novel solution requires. It's a challenge which becomes even more difficult when the context changes — with increasing rates of technological change, market demands and competitive pressures for faster development cycles and customers looking for more and more customization to their particular needs.

The role model for this is often the fast entrepreneurial start-up or small firm, quickly and nimbly dancing round the feet of lumbering giants, who are too old and set in their innovation ways to learn to move to a different tune. Those giants try in their way to recapture the entrepreneurial spark (le) of their youth — but doing so is not easy.

The place where we might expect to find some degree of entrepreneurial speed and flair is, of course, in the formal R&D/ design and development function. This is supposed to play the role of being the front-end engine of innovation for the company. Invest in this as the vehicle to drive creativity and entrepreneurial flair, make this the mode of working anyway? Except that it's often not the case. Development projects are just that — *projects* which carry high uncertainty and which we often try to control by planning and prediction. We've got some sharp tools for resource allocation — think SAP, Prince 2, etc. — but the challenge is often that we get enmeshed in the systematic way we move forward. We get there in the end but slowly and safely — and sometimes too late or with a less than dramatic solution which doesn't fully delight the customer or meet their needs.

Project management is all about anticipating and planning for risks and uncertainties and, not surprisingly, its implementation often has a built-in tendency to play safe, to review slowly and to change direction reluctantly. And the larger the scale the more controls we bring to bear, slowing and constraining innovation in the pursuit of safety and quality.

This approach is reinforced by an underlying culture in many large organizations which can remember problems when corners were cut or projects went wrong in the market place. Damage to reputation and direct costs associated with putting the problem right build up a strong resistance to taking risks and further press for control and detailed planning.

At the same time there is a sense that the organization needs to develop greater flexibility, speed, agility in handling innovation projects in a context where market needs, competitor behaviour and core technologies are changing faster than ever. There is a real push towards trying to bring a new style of working to the organization, relearn the tools and techniques of the start-up. The vision here is pretty exciting — with limited resources build a high performing team to deliver an uncertain project within a short time-scale, one which keeps investors on board and gathers momentum from initial idea to full implementation. Even a little of this magic dust might be useful — but how to bring this into the mainstream ways of working with quality standards and careful controls? And how to do this in such a way that you can repeat the trick, make a process out of the experience of a single agile project? How to distil the methods and make them a methodology which can be repeatedly applied, trained and shared across the organization?

That's the story of what has come to be called 'agile innovation' — a back to basics rethink of how to get a more entrepreneurial but still controlled approach into innovation projects.[2] It's got a fairly long history, dating back at least 30 years as a systematic and documented approach. And the accumulating evidence suggests that it works — when used appropriately (we'll return to that shortly) agile innovation contributes to:

• Higher productivity and lower cost

• Improved employee engagement and job satisfaction

• Faster time to market

• Higher quality

• Improved stakeholder satisfaction

A BRIEF HISTORY OF AGILE

Agile thinking began in the world of software development and the big challenge of failure in large-scale projects. Traditionally the idea of developing software followed a 'waterfall' model in which projects ran in sequential fashion through various different functions in the organization. Sales and marketing might identify a customer need which would then be passed to design and then to development, testing, and deployment. The whole process took a long time and there was a high risk that what emerged at the end was less than successful, either at a technical level or in terms of meeting the customer specification. On the way through this journey the project would rely on extensive controls, detailed documentation and project management according to a 'master plan' developed and worked out at the outset of the project.

Some developers began to search for alternatives and in particular Jeff Sutherland and Ken Schwaber began experimenting in the early 1990s with an approach they adapted from work on physical product development in Japan.[3] Several studies of the processes in operation there — notably by Nonaka and Takeuchi, reported in Harvard Business Review in 1986 — suggested there was a new approach based less on the idea of a sequential relay race' than a 'rugby team' metaphor, in which everyone was moving forward but in parallel and passing the ball along as they did so. This 'new innovation game' had made significant inroads to cutting development time and improving quality in projects.[4]

Sutherland and Schwaber took some of these ideas, drawing on the rugby metaphor, to create their 'scrum' approach; others worked in different ways on the same lines, with names like 'extreme programming'. In 2001 at a meeting of like-minded developers they coined the term 'agile' to describe the umbrella under which these new approaches might sit. Their work had significant impact on software projects — for example a recent survey by the management consultancy Bain and Co, reviewing 'tens of thousands of software development projects' suggested that *agile methods boosted average success rates to 39% from 11%, a more than threefold improvement. In large, complex projects agile's success rate jumps to six times that of conventional methods'*.

Whilst software development was the crucible in which the idea of agile was fused together it drew on many earlier contributing streams. For example, a key element used ideas adapted in a variety of ways around concepts of early involvement, and simultaneous or concurrent engineering. The emphasis was in trying to work in parallel, sharing relevant knowledge early and quickly and making sure all the functions involved could explore the emerging solution. Tools to help included various DfX approaches (design for manufacture, design for assembly, etc.) which tried to bring some of the downstream knowledge to bear at an early stage.

Another key idea was the concept of a dedicated team with the responsibility and authority to explore and experiment — something which had emerged in several studies during the 1990s including Wheelwright and Clark's work where they identified the 'heavyweight project manager/team' model as relevant for major innovation projects.[5] In many ways this model dates right back to the early days of the 'skunk works', an approach pioneered at Lockheed during the 1940s and based on setting up a small, dedicated team with a strong leader and the autonomy to explore their own (sometimes unconventional) route towards completing a major project within a tight schedule and with limited resources.[6]

Another important contribution came from the world of 'lean' thinking. This radically different approach to manufacturing evolved out of post-War Japan where a resource-constrained economy forced a new way of working emphasizing waste reduction. Through experiments in companies like Toyota a powerful set of principles and tools emerged which provided a disciplined methodology for working in lean fashion. They soon found application outside of manufacturing and one direction in which they were applied was in thinking about the challenge of new product development. Versions of 'lean NPD' began to emerge in many companies, and it was also very successfully transferred to the world of the start-up.[7]

LEAN START-UP

By their nature start-ups are resource-constrained operations, often trying to achieve something very different and with high potential impact. Start-ups need to experiment and explore — but if they do so carelessly they will soon run out of support and, more importantly, resources. So there is a strong underlying pressure to learn how to innovate, to move quickly but at the same time to manage and control resources carefully. An extreme version of our paradox from earlier.

Lean start-up (LSU) is an approach very similar to agile which was developed by Eric Ries and popularized by him and Steve Blank in various books and articles.[8] It draws on his own experience as an entrepreneur and his reflections on what went wrong with the process. At it's with agile innovation, at heart is the view that starting a new venture is about a series of short fast experiments rather than a carefully planned and executed big project. Each cycle is carefully designed to generate information and test ideas out on the market — and after each prototype the venture idea is adjusted. Key principles are the 'minimum viable product' (MVP) which is a simple basic version of the overall product idea which can be tested on users to gain feedback, and the 'pivot', which is changes in direction as a result of that feedback.

The origin of the 'lean' idea comes from the low waste approach pioneered in manufacturing and widely used across all sectors. It has been applied to product development to reduce time and resources spent and in software in particular has been allied to a second principle, of 'agile' development. Here the main project is broken down into a series of fast short cycles of prototypes and learning, with the development team effort concentrated in fast bursts of intense activity — the 'scrum'.

LSU developed in the field of software and web applications but the underlying philosophy can be applied in any project.

Fifty Shades of Agile

Whilst there is growing evidence for the success and value of agile approaches it is very much not a case of 'one size fits all'. There's a real risk of organizations jumping into this new approach because it seems fashionable; the evidence is that it will only help when it is adapted and configured in the right fashion.

Agile isn't a single technique but a system, a way of thinking about projects, an enabling methodology and a toolkit from which organizations can configure their own approach. It addresses many common problems in new product development so a good place to start is by understanding where current systems have weaknesses and adopting/experimenting with agile approaches to improve them.

For example major projects need to bring in many different perspectives, involve different functions all of whom contribute their expertise. The result is often a large and unwieldy team, and one in which the risks of things being missed because of the complexity of communication means that quality needs to be checked and controlled on a regular basis. Project planning is heavy at the front end, trying to anticipate all the many possible problems which might emerge and considerable efforts are spent on working with customers to ensure the specification of their needs is tightly nailed down. All the key features are designed in at the outset and then documented — again adding to the time in delivering the project because these need to be captured and detailed. And only when the entire project, with all its features is ready and checked and documented is it tested — and inevitably bugs emerge which need to be ironed out, adding further to the time and budget.

This 'heavy' front end serial model involves several stages:

- Idea→

- Features identified and discussed→

- Design→

- Develop→

- Integrate→

- Test→

- Deliver and deploy

By contrast an agile approach makes use of a small core team (which can still draw on a wider network of expertise) but on a 'just-in-time' basis. They are in constant contact with the customer, testing and checking out the development as making sure that they are only building in what is of value to the customer. Design is based on an outline and a module approach which prioritizes key design features and can adapt and add as the project develops. Development takes the form of a series of learning loops/cycles testing and fixing as they go and in particular testing out customer reaction and evaluation. Modules are added, features built in in a process of rapid short cycle improvements.

It's not a case of replacing the old project management discipline with a small team 'trust us' mentality — agile can deliver the relevant controls to fit, it relies on the same core disciplines of collaboration, testing, customer involvement, etc. But it does so in a more flexible configuration which is particularly suited to certain environments and project types.

Table 12.1 shows where agile might offer benefits: (based on Bain[9]).

It follows from this that aligning the wider organizational culture is also a key theme — it's a way of working which can easily suit start-ups but which might conflict with long-established traditions in older bigger businesses. This doesn't mean that there is no scope for agile but that some form of piloting and exploration would be needed to help learn, configure and adapt methods. For many organizations the idea of a 'spectrum' of choice of project methods is useful, running from traditional approaches at one end, through adoption of some agile practices, through to agile execution around key tasks and project phases to full agile. And in most cases there is scope for running 'hybrid' models combining agile strengths with traditional approaches.

Table 12.1. Agile and Traditional Approaches to Innovation.

Where Agile Might Help	Where Traditional Models are Appropriate
Fast changing environments and customer choice and changes in their needs and wants	Stable markets, technologies, predictable customer requirements
Risk is high, many dimensions not fully elaborated	Risk is low, project is well understood
Close collaboration where there is learning on both sides, customers discover what they value and what features really matter, co-creation	Customer specification is clear and unlikely to change. Customers may not want or may not be able and available for close collaboration
Problems are complex and solutions unknown — high uncertainty where experimentation and learning is the pattern. Relevant knowledge sets not fully defined so need cross functional collaboration/ involvement	Problems are well understood, perhaps an update along a familiar trajectory. Technologies are stable and understood, proven solutions are available, relevant knowledge sets are known and projects can run by serial/sequential involvement of different knowledge silos. Project outcomes can be clearly forecast and relevant tests and measures for quality control are available
Project lends itself to breaking down into modules. Customers can have their value in modular chunks, can change and add to their specification as they learn what would be valuable modules to add. Late changes are acceptable to basic core platform functionality. MVP and pivoting are possible and desirable	Project is indivisible into modules so can't be tested and checked until fully built. Late changes are expensive or impossible. MVP is the final product, no pivoting possible
Mistakes can be found and rectified in the next development cycle — fast failure mode and extensive in process learning	Interim mistakes have big negative impact so detailed testing and checking at every stage is required.
Suited to team-based collaborative culture with extensive horizontal/process flow of knowledge	Suited to top-down control environments and specialist functional knowledge silos

WHAT'S IN THE AGILE TOOL BOX?

It's worth lifting the lid on some of the more common agile tools to get a sense of how they might contribute to faster and more flexible product development.

Agile innovation has evolved into a suite of methods which have been increasingly applied outside of software development to other new products, services and even process re-engineering. At its heart is an approach which emphasizes focused high intensity team work (often called a 'scrum'), stretching goals and rapid cycles of prototyping, testing and learning. Where conventional project management techniques set a goal and then break down the various tasks needed to complete it into key activities and allocate resources to them agile methods are more open-ended, allowing considerable creativity and flexibility in the execution of activities which will move nearer to the stretch target.

The basic framework in an agile approach involves setting up a core self-managed team, drawing on different functions and with a clear and stretching target. The team use various creativity tools (such as brainstorming and design thinking) to generate a list of key features which they think will be of value to the end user. Two key roles operate — a team leader who represents the end user's point of view and ranks these features from that perspective, and a process facilitator whose role is to help manage the support and psychological safety aspects of the team.

Once the stretch goal (vision) is broken down into a ranked list of contributing projects the team work on short problem solving cycles ('sprints') around these issues. Typically there is a short review meeting at the start of each day to explore progress, challenge and strengthen ideas and develop experiments which they then test out during the day. The results of those experiments provide feedback and data to fuel the next day's review meeting and drive the sprint forward. Experiments may be of a technical nature — for example writing code or developing a working prototype — or they may be market tests, trying out the ideas with potential end users. In both cases the idea is to move through a fast cycle of experiment and learn, with the prospect of failure seen simply as a learning opportunity rather than a block to further progress.

To enable such an approach there needs to be a core team and they often have a physical space set aside — a 'war room' is an analogy often used here — in which progress can be tracked, scrum meetings held and each day's activities planned and reviewed.

Some useful additions to the agile repertoire come from the world of lean start-up, including the following:

Build-Measure-Learn

The principle here is to design a hypothesis to test an idea and then adjust the project on the basis of that feedback. So, for example, it can be used to test a particular feature where the hypothesis is that people will like and value it; if they do then retain the feature, if they don't, drop it.

Minimum Viable Product (MVP)

This is the minimum configuration of the new venture idea which can be used to run a build/measure/learn cycle — a simple prototype whose purpose is to generate data which helps adjust the core idea for the venture.

Validated Learning

An important element of LSU is to work with data which provides useful information and helps learning about the venture. Ries talks about the problem of 'vanity metrics' which might appear to be measures of success but don't actually reveal anything useful. The number of people visiting a web-page for example is not helpful in itself but the amount of time they spend or the features they click on may be because it gives information about the underlying things that people are valuing — at least enough to send some time on. Equally the number of return visitors is a useful metric.

Innovation Accounting

Linked to validated learning is the idea of using data to ensure resources are being well spent. To do this requires establishing a baseline and then improving on the performance linked to that by varying elements in the MVP — a process Ries calls 'tuning the engine'. For example a simple baseline could be set by a market survey which asks people if they would buy a product or service. Then launching an MVP cycle would generate data which suggested that more (or less) of them would be interested — and the core concept could be pivoted before a re-test cycle. In this way the scarce resources associated with innovation can be carefully tracked.

Pivoting

The core assumption in LSU is that the only way to get closer to what customers actually need is to test your idea out on them and adapt it according to feedback from several learning cycles. So there is a need to use data from experiments to adjust the offer — the idea of a pivot is not that you change the idea completely but pivot it around the core so that it more exactly meets market needs. YouTube was originally a dating site on which one of the many features offered was the ability to share short video clips. During MVP tests it became clear that this feature was particularly valued so the original idea was adapted to put this more up front; further tests showed it was sufficiently valued to make it the core feature of the new business venture.

The essence of pivoting and MVP could be summed up as 'launch and see what happens' — inevitably something will and if the experimental launch is well designed it will help sharpen and refine the final offering without too much resource waste. Even if the MVP is a 'failure' there is valuable learning about new directions in which to pivot.

Ries talks about several versions of the pivot:

- *Zoom-in pivot*, where a single feature in the product now becomes the entire product (as in the YouTube case).

- *Zoom-out pivot*, where the whole product becomes a single feature in something much larger.

- *Customer segment pivot*, where the product was right, but the original customer segment wasn't. By rethinking the customer target segment the product can be better positioned.

- *Customer need pivot*, where validated learning highlights a more important customer need or problem.

- *Platform pivot*, where single separate applications converge to become a platform.

- *Business architecture pivot*, essentially changing the underlying business model — for example from high margin, low volume, to low margin, high volume.

- *Value capture pivot*, where changes involve rethinking marketing strategy, cost structure, product, etc.

- *Engine of growth pivot*, where the start-up model is rethought. Ries suggests three core models for this — viral, sticky, or paid growth — and there is scope to change between them.

- *Channel pivot*, where different routes to reach the market are explored.

- *Technology pivot*, where alternative new technologies are used but the rest of the business model — market, cost structure, etc. — remains the same.

Single Unit Flow

An idea which originated in the Toyota Production System and is one of the cornerstones of 'lean' thinking. In essence it is about working in small batches and completing the tasks on those rather than working in high volume. Think about doing a mailshot which would involve stuffing envelopes, addressing them, stamping them, posting them, etc. Doing this in high volume one task at a time runs the risk of being slow and also of errors being made and not detected — for example spelling someone's name wrong. Working one unit at a time would be faster and more accurate.

Applied to LSU the idea is to work at small scale to develop the system and identify errors and problems quickly; the whole system can then be redesigned to take out these problems.

Line Stop/Andon Cord

Another idea drawn from Toyota is the ability to stop production when an error occurs — in the giant car factories this is done by means of a cord and a light which flashes above the place where the employee has found a problem. In LSU it is the principle of making sure there are error checks and that the process is stopped until these are fixed.

Continuous Improvement

Another Toyota-based principle which is to keep reviewing and improving the core product and the process delivering it. By working in small batches (see section 'Single Unit Flow') it is possible to experiment and optimize around the core idea.

Kanban

Yet another 'lean' feature this refers to the system of stock management associated with just-in-time production. Applied to LSU it puts improvement projects around the core product/venture idea into 'buckets' which are processed and progressed in systematic fashion. It is a powerful aid to managing capacity since new projects cannot be started until there is room for them in the system.

Five Whys

As a powerful diagnostic tool this helps find root causes of problems and directs action towards solving those problems rather than treating symptoms.

MAKING AGILE INNOVATION WORK

Like any good idea the test comes in the implementation; much depends on configuring an appropriate model for a particular organization rather than assuming here is a single 'plug and play' version of agile. Research suggest several areas where agile projects often run aground:

a. Lack of understanding. Agile is still evolving and the risk is that it is adopted as a fashion accessory without a deeper understanding of where and why as well as how.

b. Lack of skills/experience — in a survey by Bain and Co 44% of respondents blame failure on lack of familiarity with agile methods with another 35% saying that there are not enough personnel with the necessary experience.

c. Lack of management support, often stemming from concerns about losing control of projects.

d. Agile principles at odds with the company's operating model. As we have seen agile approaches challenge much of the plan and control culture and moving to models like scrum may not fit with the dominant project culture for innovation.

e. Trying to fit agile elements into non-agile framework.

These are not surprising and they suggest an approach which recognizes the need to develop an understanding and the relevant skills and to pilot before attempting to spread across the whole organization.

The good news is that there is an emerging pathway to successful implementation with a number of guidelines on the roadmap. These include:

- Build on the principles and adapt/evolve the practices. Just like lean there is a small set of well-proven ideas at the heart and then a variety of enabling tools and techniques, not all of which will work in different situations. It's also about learning to use those tools, building capability around a new way of working with innovation.

- Use a pilot and learn approach rather than a 'big bang'. This aligns with the above point about acquiring the skills and capability, plus it allows for the organization to have a 'mixed economy' — not every project fits the agile template. The value of starting small is that a team can be built who can become evangelists and experts to help spread the principles; whilst external support might be needed early on to teach the principles and tools this can quickly be internalized. In addition pilots provide an opportunity to collect data which can help convince sceptics that the approach can work in our particular company context.

- Work with matrix/temporary models of structure rather than change the whole organization. Agile isn't for all projects and there may well be a strong argument for maintaining knowledge concentrated in functions. But within agile teams allow for a different mode of working which emphasizes fast cross functional sharing, collaboration, shared experimentation, etc.

- Create psychological safety — agile teams work differently and have much in common with 'skunk works' — the sense of being able to experiment and fail fast. This requires team members to trust each other but also an external sense that they are 'licensed' to experiment and play.

- Build the team — invest in teambuilding to enable high performance creativity. Key in agile is facilitation and support — central role of scrum master. Reward and recognition become more intrinsic.

- Measurement frameworks — may need to adapt to value different KPIs but eventually also need to align with bigger picture.

- Give autonomy and heavyweight project management authority. Key part of the model is the war room and fast-focused decision-making — can't be constantly referring outside and upwards. Clear lines around decision authority and remit and autonomy within them.

WHY AGILE MATTERS FOR HELLA

For a company like Hella innovation is essential — it's one of the first words in the Annual Report, it's part of the company DNA. But with it comes a need to balance — innovation is about taking risks and exploring but it also about delivering. Much of Hella's impressive spend on innovation — close to 10% of turnover on R&D and around a fifth of their employees involved in it — is linked to major projects with clients. Big partners in the car industry, big projects in which there is a lot at stake.

For this reason the systems for managing design and development have become increasingly important as ways of controlling and managing risks, ensuring delivery and success. But with this has come an increasingly systematic mind-set, a sense of doing things inside a slow but steady machine.

Outside the world is changing. Technologies have much to offer but rates of change are increasing. Customers can define expectations but then find themselves wanting more, engineering changes, newer features, and customization. The pressure for a more agile approach is certainly there — and it needs to be linked to a context in which Hella also has to find ways of projecting an image of being innovative, not just in its product technologies but in the ways it creates and delivers those e-offerings.

There are also important external reference points; agile is a 'hot topic' in industry conferences and major competitors are making a feature of it in their sales presentations and technology road-shows.

WHAT HELLA IS DOING

Experimenting with the concept began around 2013, not least with the arrival of Michael Jaeger to head up the Electronics Division's innovation activities. With a background at Bosch he had first-hand experience of some of these approaches and quickly found some kindred spirits across the organization. An i-Circle discussion on the theme gave senior managers an insight into the principles of agile — but also range some alarm bells about the conflict between this mode of working and the current dominant company model. Whatever else, agile was a challenge to a culture where 'the way we do things round here' didn't normally extend to small teams working autonomously and emphasizing learning fast — even if it meant failing fast! Control and planning was what had built the company's innovation reputation there was too much at stake to jeopardize it with a new fashion.

An internal team of champions began working in 2016 with external consultants to review and help build Hella's capability in agile methods. After 3 months of working with agile in several project areas in the United States, Germany and Romania an internal survey suggested that it offered significant improvements in:

- Job satisfaction
- Team spirit

- Project visibility
- Management of project risks
- Co-ordination with other teams and roles
- Co-ordination within team
- Work progress transparency
- Productivity
- Development processes applicability
- Quality of work results
- Time to deliver
- Personal skills
- Change and priorities management

So far 14 projects have been completed and there are a further 6 running pilots; the aim is now to capture initial learning and codify Hella's version of an agile approach. Importantly this would provide a roadmap but also flexibility for configuring different versions of agile for different situations — building the basis of a Hella capability in this important area.

FURTHER RESOURCES

You can find a number of useful resources — case studies, video and audio and tools to explore some of the themes discussed in this chapter at www.innovation-portal.info

In particular:

- Case studies of organizations taking an agile approach to innovation — for example in the turbulent conditions around
  humanitarian innovation or in the operations of 'skunk works'
  type groups

- Tools and frameworks (like lean start-up) to help explore themes raised in the chapter

REFLECTION QUESTIONS

1. At first sight lean/agile approaches seem to be essential to enable innovation in organizations. But there are limits to their applicability and occasions when a more structured approach will be of value. Using examples try to identify the conditions under which lean/agile would be appropriate and explain why.

2. Choose an organization with which you are familiar. Where do they need more agility in their innovation processes? Where do standards help and where do they get in the way?

3. You've been asked as consultants to advise a company on how it might develop a culture of 'intelligent failure' — that is, able to learn fast from experiments. What advice would you give in terms of structures, skills and tools which they might implement?

NOTES

1. Drucker (1985).
2. Morris, Ma, and Wu (2014).
3. Rigby, Sutherland, and Takeuchi (2016a).
4. Takeuchi and Nonaka (1986).
5. Wheelwright and Clark (1992).
6. Rich and Janos (1994).
7. Womack and Jones (1996).
8. Ries (2011) and Blank (2013).
9. Rigby et al. (2016b).

13

LOOKING TO THE FUTURE

Figure 13.1. Core Elements in Long-term Innovation.

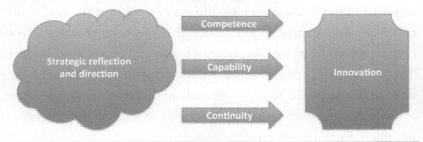

Throughout this book we've been using a simple model to help think about innovation — creating value from knowledge. It doesn't just happen — whilst luck might play a part long-term survival mostly reflects careful and strategic management. In particular it depends on three key elements (**Figure 13.1**):

- Competence — building up the knowledge base, organizing and managing its deployment, strategically targeting new directions, harvesting value from the investment.

- Capability — creating and updating the organization's innovation routines — the 'programs' which allow it to create value from the knowledge base.

- Continuity — embedding the key routines into a framework which can be passed on over time — the 'innovation DNA' of the organization.

THE PAST

We've seen the ways in which these have evolved over Hella's 120-year history — how a core knowledge base around lighting and control has been built into a position of technological leadership.

And we've also seen that whilst there is an important element of growing the knowledge base through investment the real ability to create and capture value from that investment comes from organizing and establishing routines to make innovation happen. These structures, processes and policies enable innovation these days across a broad front — embedded in products and services, in business and technological processes, in market positions and in underlying business models.

Above all we've seen continuity in this, a consistency of themes and underlying values and beliefs. Principles like 'entrepreneurial responsibility' are not simple slogans, they represent deep-rooted values about how innovation takes place and the key role which people play in the process. The innovation DNA isn't random, it has been carefully engineered and modified over time through a process of reflection and strategic experimentation, trying to get the best fit between the routines for enabling innovation and the environment in which the company is operating.

THE PRESENT

In the later parts of the book we looked at a number of examples of Hella's current 'genetic engineering' — its strategic reflections about clusters of innovation routines and where and how they could be modified or where new 'genetic material' might be spliced in to improve the company's innovation fitness.

We've seen that old patterns still work but may need 'switching on' in some areas. The Continuous Improvement story is a good example, building on a set of routines which were originally developed during the 1990s in response to a survival crisis. The model was very effective in helping work through the 'Lopez years' and made a significant contribution to Hella's improving competitive position as it entered the 21st Century. But whilst the model has persisted in many areas (especially around operations in manufacturing) there is scope for extending its application into other fields. Current work with some of the company's core processes is not only about process re-design but also about engaging a culture of continuous improvement — one that depends on spreading the enabling routines.

And we've also seen where new routines might be appropriate in key areas — but where there is a need to splice this genetic material in carefully. Agile approaches seem to offer the Holy Grail of faster and more effective new product development, building on ideas originally developed around lean start-up and software engineering. But whilst some of the tools and underlying approaches (like rapid prototyping cycles and scrum/sprint models) may have relevance they are not always appropriate. One size doesn't fit all and simply inserting a new gene for agile innovation without tailoring it to Hella's circumstances is unlikely to work.

We've also seen the continuing expression of key 'genes' — for example in the routines around platform thinking. Right back in 1908 (with the introduction of the Hella System combining headlight, lens, reflector foil) Hella was already thinking about product platforms as a way of leveraging knowledge assets — and to do this required organizing the underlying knowledge architecture and enabling people to work to support that. Today's platforms in LEDs, in body control or customer comfort modules, etc., reflect this and their successful implementation owes much to working with these well-established innovation routines.

The same goes for open innovation — the realization in the 1990s that the demands of an increasingly complex marketplace meant that competitiveness within the sector was becoming increasingly knowledge-based. But even with its strong record of investment in building competence (e.g. through sustained R&D spending) Hella was unable to cover all the knowledge territory and needed to amplify its competence. Recognition that *'not all the smart guys work for us'* drove a strategy based on new routines associated with building strategic alliances and joint ventures or targeting key acquisitions and then managing the subtle task of absorbing the new knowledge into Hella's bloodstream without destroying it.

That same set of routines are now critically important in Hella's current environment where it is trying to explore a long and exciting frontier of new technological and market possibilities. It's clear the game is changing and how to find new partners, form working relationships with them and eventually grow a new generation of high performing strategic networks is becoming a key issue.

As Hella moves into new spaces — for example through its Hella Ventures activities in Silicon Valley and Berlin — it has a major advantage in being able to draw on routines established 20 years earlier.

Of course part of the story involves areas where completely new routines might need to be spliced in to enhance capability — for example in dealing with disruptive innovation. Hella has a long history of venturing, the entrepreneurial spirit driving attempts to open up new geographical activities and to explore adjacent and speciality markets. And sometimes this has led to creating new units within the organization — that's very much been the history behind the 'Special Applications' division, for example. Hella Industries was another attempt to extend Hella's activities into new market spaces outside the automotive sector and this venture provided some valuable learning about moves of this kind.

But the scale of the potential threats or opportunities around 'disruptive innovation' mean that Hella needs to look for an organized and systematic approach to build new routines to work in this space. Establishing the Hella Ventures activity with facilities in Silicon Valley and in Berlin is the (relatively) simple part of the story, putting in place people and space in which new ways of working can emerge. The hard part is in building the routines which will eventually become 'the way we do things around here' in this area. This involves considerable experimentation, using new approaches like lean start up, new techniques like minimum viable product and pivoting and finding new ways of finding, forming and creating performing networks. This activity is essentially about trying to find new ways to express entrepreneurial behaviour and to push the envelope within which this happens — to help Hella climb out of its particular box.

We've also seen laboratory-style observation and evaluation of new routines, potential genes which could be of value for Hella to splice in. A good example here would be frugal innovation — a set of routines around thinking and working in very lean fashion, using minimum resources. This approach has considerable potential application for some of the market contexts in which Hella is increasingly working, such as India, China and Latin America. But it may also offer some challenging new ways of working back in the mainstream; it raises the possibility of 'reverse innovation' and, more important, challenges some of the fundamental values on which the company's technological strength has been based.

At the heart of Hella's innovation success has been the channelling of entrepreneurial efforts by a wide variety of people. Finding ways to tap into this sense of entrepreneurial responsibility has led to exploration of new routes around employee engagement. Whilst innovation already operates effectively along established routes and through existing structures there is also a search for parallel channels which can open up the activity. Increasing use of collaboration platforms (like the Driving e-novation contests) to source ideas and to help with their selection and downstream implementation involves learning and embedding a new set of routines but holds out considerable promise for wider engagement across a global organization.

THE FUTURE?

Standing still is never an option in innovation — it involves a moving target and, as we have seen, organizations need to take a strategic view on this, identifying emerging threats and opportunities in their future and developing responses in advance. So what are the challenges on Hella's horizon, and what might these mean for actions to retain their innovation edge?

Competence

Hella's knowledge base has grown significantly since the early days of simple lamps and horns. The company has been a major investor in R&D (maintaining close to 10% of sales as a reinvestment figure) and it has a significant proportion — close to 20% — of its workforce engaged in formal innovation activity. Through routines like CI and the increasing use of collaboration platforms this commitment is likely to increase.

Three questions in particular emerge in this space.

Entry into Major New Technological Fields

Whilst it had a small presence in the field of electronics dating back to the 1960s Hella made a major strategic commitment in the 1980s to embrace electronics as a key field. This was not easy at the time — the technology was immature, the skills available to explore it were scarce and there were few facilities within the company to enable its adaptation and development into useful innovations. As we saw in Chapter 4 Hella took some big risks and relied heavily on internal entrepreneurship to make this move work — but it paid off. Today's strong business position owes a great deal to the strategic decisions taken 40 years ago to move into new technological territory.

It's commonplace today to talk about 'the internet of things' — a world in which intelligence is built into everyday experience in the home, the car, the office, the factory, wherever human beings find themselves. It is enabled by thousands of smart devices — sensors and actuators — communicating with controllers and networks creating a context of intelligent applications. And underpinning this is not only the advanced technology with which Hella is familiar — sensors and actuators — but also machine learning. Artificial intelligence as a concept dates back to the 1970s but its realization has been held back by hardware and software limitations and by the lack of a clear pathway to enable learning applications. Problems could be solved by using brute force — chess playing computers which relied on calculating every possible move and then choosing the best. But developments which drew heavily on neuroscience have given us a new generation of machines capable of learning and inferring for themselves the rules and then the effective strategies for dealing with unknown situations. In working their way along this route they emulate the processes human beings use — and many commentators argue that we are close to an inflection point where machine learning has come of age and can replace human activity in multiple situations.

Google's Deep Mind managed to consistently beat the world's champion at the game of 'Go' a strategy based challenge which is generally acknowledge to be much more difficult than chess. And Libratus, a program developed at Carnegie-Mellon University took on 4 poker champions over a period of 20 days in a Pittsburgh casino and walked away the winner with nearly €2m in chips! The significance of this is that it represents an ability to work with imperfect information — poker is a game in which strategy is combined with emotional judgments and behaviours like bluffing. In order to achieve this machine intelligence needs to have what psychologists call a 'theory of mind' — the ability to imagine what someone else is thinking and to use that simulation to devise strategies for working with, or defeating them. Evolutionary psychologists equate the emergence of this ability in humans to the point at which 'imagination' became possible and from which much subsequent creative activity can be traced.

Today's machine learning algorithms and applications are still relatively simple but they are rushing up a learning curve and finding application in an increasing number of contexts. This represents a major threat or opportunity for Hella (and one of the major areas of work within the berlin Ventures organization is exploring many different machine learning applications). But such technology is also likely to have major impacts on the quality and quantity of employment and so for Hella the challenge of future *process* innovation will be increasingly bound up with it.

The strategic implication is that for the kind of business which Hella has become, increasingly talking about 'intelligence' and 'sense' in a 'connected world', the move into machine learning may not simply be the next step along an established trajectory but instead require the kind of investment and commitment which the 1980s move into electronics represented.

Where and How Hella Uses its Knowledge Base

And particularly, in a world of open innovation, where and how it might trade with that. In the past the challenge has been one of managing a careful fit between the needs of automotive and adjacent markets and developing the technology to meet those needs. But increasingly the potential scope for a sensing/actuating company extends beyond this and into the wider 'internet of things'.

Knowledge for any organization is its key asset. Kodak is an example — a company which was dominant in the 20th Century but disrupted by the shifts in technology and by the ways in which digital imaging became used. But Kodak is not dead — it survives and is growing again on the basis of re-deploying some of its core knowledge assets in new fields, especially in high-speed printing. A less dramatic story in terms of the crisis ending is that of Fujifilm, once a rival to Kodak in the old world of film-based photography. Fuji was able to move across into a number of different fields deploying its deep technological competence to enter new markets like cosmetics.

There are challenges and opportunities in moving to new areas of knowledge application. At one end of the spectrum is the increasingly busy open innovation marketplace in which knowledge is traded — licensing, buying and selling of non-core technological assets, strategic alliances and joint ventures are all part of this game. And it is one which Hella has played effectively, although its past successes in open innovation have been around using the open innovation market to amplify its own technological capabilities. In the future there may be significant opportunities for Hella to become a seller of technology — but doing so will require developing capabilities around strategic IP management and venturing models based on trying to harvest good yields form technology investments.

At the limit there is, of course, the possibility of growth through extending the footprint of application for Hella's knowledge base. This is difficult because it requires learning new rules and strategies to enter very different markets. Hella's attempt to do this with Hella Industries provided some valuable lessons about how difficult such a move can be — but the underlying business rationale was correct. For an increasingly knowledge-rich company finding the navigation skills to once again launch into new waters may be an important next step.

Maintaining Momentum

Hella began life as a product-based company and quickly realized the competitive advantage which technological knowledge could bring. Investment in what we would recognize as R&D began very early — and has clearly paid dividends for the company. At the same time the level of investment is high — close to 10% of turnover ploughed back into the knowledge base and close to one fifth of the workforce linked to innovation. Maintaining this level of commitment, especially in the face of an external capital market which will increasingly look to see this justified, is going to be a challenge. Part of the answer to this may lie in redefining Hella as a technology company rather than a lighting, electronics player.

Capability

A simple model to aid reflection around innovation routines is given below and it raises some key questions which any organization should ask itself — and keep on asking (**Figure 13.2**).

The preceding section has shown some of the ways in which Hella is exploring key themes which represent new or modified innovation capabilities. In its efforts at 'genetic engineering' — ensuring that the right strands of innovation DNA are passed

Figure 13.2. A Model of the Innovation Process.

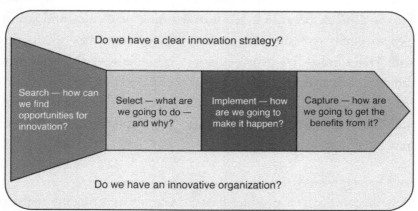

on — there is a need for constant review, modification and splicing in of new behaviours.

For example in the area of 'agile' innovation there is much going on to adapt the approaches which have demonstrable potential in other organizations. Faster cycles of new product development and greater demands for customization require flexible processes — but at the same time Hella's core business requires huge investments in new product generation and so their development needs to be carefully and closely managed. Striking the balance and absorbing new genetic material (the ideas emerging from the agile pilots) is going to be critical to the future.

By contrast the challenge around continuous improvement is how to refresh the gene. Twenty years ago some very effective new approaches were introduced into the innovation repertoire but recent experience has seen their effectiveness decline and they remain concentrated in key areas of the business but have not spread elsewhere. Here the innovation capability development is around capturing the essence of the effective gene and then exploring variants which can work in different contexts. In particular they accompany a wholesale review of corporate management processes which should mean that CI is applied to improving the right processes and engaging people's entrepreneurial responsibility in support of that.

Platform thinking is another area where Hella has proven and effective routines and these offer powerful routes to leverage the expensive knowledge base which the company has accumulated over decades. Carefully understanding the core routines and ensuring that the things which make platform thinking work — like mobilizing cross-functional flow of ideas and close collaboration with end-users — will be essential to a future role as a knowledge-based business.

There are new challenges. Extending the idea of high involvement, of allowing more participation in the entrepreneurial thinking of the company has been limited in the past by the problems of managing idea flow, resource allocation and alignment with business strategy. But new approaches are being explored outside by large international organizations, using collaboration platforms to build thriving entrepreneurial communities. Hella's exploration of idea contests, using gamification to help draw in a wide range of participants and encouraging targeted attention to key challenge areas has been a largely positive experience.

Mobilizing this for the long term requires a supportive context. At the minimum it needs an IT infrastructure capable of supporting increasingly powerful collaboration software — but it also needs an organizational infrastructure. Large players like Airbus or Siemens have a team of staff whose role is to support the innovation process and enable people to express their creativity and enthusiasm for both improvement and for radical breakthrough innovation. In many ways this represents a 21st Century version of the challenge to senior management around entrepreneurial responsibility — creating the conditions and structures within which people are enabled to deliver that.

The question of 'frugal' innovation is interesting. On the one hand it offers an interesting perspective on the ways in which we think about innovation. It is certainly appropriate to contexts where there are resource constraints and to markets with less purchasing power. And for this reason alone it may well be important for Hella to build on growing understanding and practices using the laboratories which its operations in India and China represent.

But frugal is also a way of thinking along different innovation trajectories, not simply reducing complex technology to cheap cheerful lower specification variants. It is more about distillation, refining concepts and delivering them in an elegant configuration; it allows for complexity to be added back in using the kind of platform-plus-modules approach which is already familiar in Hella. Powerful tools which Hella recognizes — the 'lean approaches underpinning the Hella Production System', the value engineering already used in product development — are at the heart of frugal thinking. But frugal thinking also requires a willingness to think about radical alternatives to the dominant paradigm — the mental model within the business. The core values of technical excellence delivered in the form of high specification solutions at (relatively) high cost may be challenged in a future where growth is increasingly likely to come in emerging nations where more frugal approaches may be appropriate.

Finally there is the emerging frontier along which Hella now needs to work. An industry with which it was familiar is now moving to a new fluid state, de-maturing as new technologies, competitors and market conditions swirl around. To work in this space requires the capacity to act entrepreneurially, to probe and learn, to experiment and fail. It requires new networks to be built and new ways of developing business ideas and testing them out to become part of the 'way we do things around here'. The Hella Ventures initiative has made an important start and has already begun to yield important lessons for further development of these new routines. The question here for the future is twofold; first what additional capabilities might be needed and second, how to ensure that these new routines can connect back into the mainstream innovation infrastructure across Hella.

In terms of the first question Hella ventures has established two important bridgeheads, providing a scouting and network-building capability in a key location (Silicon Valley) and learning how to operate a fast and agile corporate venture group in berlin. Given the rapid changes and the importance of regional contexts and contacts there may well be scope to extend the Silicon Valley model to other regions — for example in India or China. And whilst the Berlin operation has already begun to bring back potential business opportunities which can be leveraged in new business hosted by parts of the mainstream company there may be scope for extending the range of venturing activity.

Intel, for example, engages in 'eco-system venturing' alongside its corporate venture group. Here some of the start-ups in the space surrounding its emerging business interests are identified and venture funding and other forms of support is made available to enable these seeds to grow into what Intel sees as likely to be key network partners in its future ecosystem. Whilst at the moment some of the fringe start-ups in Berlin may appear to have little to do with today's Hella they could be important elements in a future puzzle — and finding ways to connect with them and possibly grow with them might be a useful addition to the venturing strategy.

Research on corporate venturing suggests that many companies recognize the need to augment their mainstream innovation capability with a more entrepreneurial element at the edge. But for many of these ventures the evidence it that it is *'a short life but a happy one'*. There are real tensions which quickly emerge around the relationship with the main organization — trying to balance enough distance and freedom to operate outside the main planet without spinning off into deep space, never to return! There are issues around funding and the opportunity costs involved in committing resources to uncertain exploration of the future. And there are different attitudes around risk levels, autonomy and control. All of which often result in the withdrawal of support and sometimes the closure of the venture.

These are typical stages in the life cycle of new venture organizations and Hella is aware of the need to manage the growth and integration of Hella Ventures carefully. Regular reviews and workshops exploring both the content and importantly the underlying processes help to keep a sense of strategic alignment. In addition they develop the pathways to the main body of the company, opening important knowledge channels and building a sense of connection.

Continuity

One of the things we have explored in this book is the concept of Hella's innovation DNA — the ways in which it carries forward the particular values and behaviours over time. It's clear this is not simply a useful phrase to put in the Annual Report but a very real strand which does run through its history. It is embedded in the 'genes' — the routines which the company has developed and which it passes on, expressing 'the way we do things around here' and shaping the behaviour of the future organization.

And we've also seen the key role played by strategic leadership in managing this. Making the values explicit and reinforcing them at key stages is critical, 'walking the talk' so that these are not seen as simple slogans but actually describe the way the organization works. They become the story it tells to itself, and the messages it passes on to new employees who join the company. Concepts like 'the Hella family' are a part of this, themes like 'entrepreneurial responsibility' run deep in the organization's psyche.

But there is also an important role around reviewing, reflecting and refining the routines — the genetic material which carries the message forward. Challenging the ways things have worked, modifying and adapting routines and, of critical importance, introducing new strands as the environment places new challenges on the organization.

We have seen this at key points in the past — for example:

i. the reorganization of electronics and particularly product development there during the 1990s.

ii. the response to the huge challenges posed during the 'Lopez years' and the significant mobilization of continuous improvement routines across the organization.

iii. the shift to a network strategy, anticipating the era of 'open innovation' in recognizing that 'not all the smart guys work for us' and actively pursuing key strategic links with other knowledge partners.

iv. the setting up of Hella ventures as a targeted response to the potential challenges and opportunities around disruptive innovation.

And the future survival and growth of Hella as an innovative leader in its industry will depend on maintaining this strategic leadership. How can the 'dynamic capability' — the capacity to step back, reflect and then revise the innovation DNA of the organization — be maintained?

One answer, of course, is via the leadership of the company. Hella has been fortunate in having experienced and committed leaders at each stage in its evolution, and the strong family ties have helped maintain support and continuity for what were sometimes difficult strategic decisions. In more recent time this leadership role has been played by the 'double act' of Jürgen Behrend and Rolf Breidenbach, bringing complementary skills and experience and managing to balance the dimensions of exploration and operation. There has been a creative tension between pushing in new directions, stretching Hella's more radical innovation activity and maintaining strong operational excellence, founded on a steady stream of continuous incremental innovation. It would be an oversimplification to say that each took one specific role but it is clear that the process of strategic development of Hella's innovation routines — its DNA — owes much to their interplay.

With Jürgen Behrend's retirement in 2017 comes a challenge around maintaining that momentum. How will the strategic issues be surfaced, explored and debated? How will the entrepreneurial spirit, pushing into new approaches, be balanced with the increasing pressures coming from external stakeholders in a public company to maintain steady growth and operational excellence?

KEEPING THE INNOVATION CONVERSATION GOING

As we have seen, innovation is central to Hella's successful growth and maintaining this momentum requires continuing reflection and exploration of the theme and how best to organize for innovation. To do so means having regular and sustained 'conversations', allowing for discussion and debate about this core element. One mechanism which has played a useful role in doing so and arguably in shaping recent thinking at strategic levels has been the i-Circle. As a regular (bimonthly) place where informal exploration, discussion and elaboration of innovation challenges can be explored it has been useful. In the preceding section we have seen how many of the current initiatives around enhancing or extending Hella's innovation routines — its 'genetic engineering' of its innovation DNA — have begun within i-Circle meetings. They represent an important cross-divisional and cross-functional place where networking and experience sharing can take place and where there is a sustained 'conversation with innovation' as part of the formal agenda. The model also allows for an external perspective, for windows to be opened on the experience of other organizations — Siemens, Nokia, Airbus have been recent visitors — and for examination of important new technological and social trends. In essence it creates a community of practice around innovation.

There may be scope for extending the model, bringing in other areas and levels into the discussion. Or communicating the discussion more widely — one opportunity in a collaboration platform is to create the space, the forum within which such discussions can be explored and opinions and ideas shared.

But there may also be scope for extending the repertoire through which Hella conducts such conversations about innovation. Its long history of successfully 'breeding' its innovation DNA has so far relied on a model of direct leadership with senior managers taking a key role. Their critical reflection and capability building insights and initiatives have been fitted alongside their other responsibilities. But with significant innovation-led growth comes a problem of managerial attention and there may now be a case for augmenting top team oversight of innovation capability with some more operational capacity for its exploration and development.

Questions of competence development — managing the knowledge base — remain critical but these are explored and agreed upon in discussion with many players. Increasingly large international organizations similar to Hella have taken an approach to the development of innovation capability which uses some form of specialist support team/function to enable it. The remit of such teams varies but picks up many of the themes we have been discussing in the book, putting them on a more systematic organization-wide footing. For example:

- organizing 'conversations about innovation', keeping the topic in people's minds and allowing exploration and exchange of ideas and experience,

- supporting the roll-out of innovation contests, campaigns and other activities on a collaboration platform,

- providing direct support for key initiatives — things like the Continuous Improvement or Agile work currently going on within Hella,

- building external networks (academic, industrial, public policy) for sharing experiences and tools, techniques, etc., in innovation management.

Their role is essentially catalytic and one value is their ability to spread good practices and concentrate the knowledge base around innovation capability. As this book has tried to show Hella has learned a lot more about effective innovation management than it sometimes believes, and also has much more experience in this domain than it shares.

REFERENCES

Abernathy, W., & Utterback, J. (1975). A dynamic model of product and process innovation. *Omega, 3*(6), 639–656.

Afuah, A. (2003). *Business models: A strategic management approach*. New York, NY: McGraw Hill.

Allen, T. (1977). *Managing the flow of technology*. Cambridge, MA: MIT Press.

Altschuler, D., Roos, D., Jones, D., & Womack, D. (1984). *The future of the automobile*. Cambridge, MA: MIT Press.

Bahghai, M., Coley, S., & White, D. (1999). *The alchemy of growth*. New York, NY: Perseus Publishing.

Bessant, J. (2003). *High involvement innovation*. Chichester: Wiley.

Bessant, J. (2017). *A maturity model for high involvement innovation*. Bonn: Hype Software. Retrieved from http://www.hypeinnovation.com/home

Bessant, J., Caffyn, S., & Gallagher, M. (2001). An evolutionary model of continuous improvement behaviour. *Technovation, 21*(3), 67–77.

Bessant, J., & Moeslein, K. (2011). *Open collective innovation*. London: AIM – Advanced Institute of Management Research.

Bessant, J., & Tidd, J. (2015). *Innovation and entrepreneurship*. Chichester: Wiley.

Birkinshaw, J., Bessant, J., & Delbridge, R. (2007). Finding, forming, and performing: Creating networks for discontinuous innovation. *California Management Review*, 49(3), 67–83.

Birkinshaw, J., & Gibson, C. (2004). Building ambidexterity into an organization. *Sloan Management Review*, 45(4), 47–55.

Blank, S. (2013). Why the lean start-up changes everything. *Harvard Business Review*, 91(5), 63–72.

Boer, H., Berger, A., Chapman, R., & Gertsen, F. (1999). *CIchanges: From suggestion box to the learning organisation.* Aldershot: Ashgate.

Buckland, W., Hatcher, A., & Birkinshaw, J. (2003). *Inventuring: Why big companies must think small.* London: McGraw Hill Business.

Burt, R. (2005). *Brokerage and closure.* Oxford: Oxford University Press.

Chesbrough, H. (2003). *Open innovation: The new imperative for creating and profiting from technology.* Boston, MA: Harvard Business School Press.

Christensen, C. (1997). *The innovator's dilemma.* Cambridge, MA: Harvard Business School Press.

Day, G., & Schoemaker, P. (2006). *Peripheral vision: Detecting the weak signals that will make or break your company.* Boston, MA: Harvard Business School Press.

de Geus, A. (1996). *The living company.* Boston, MA: Harvard Business School Press.

Deming, W. E. (1986). *Out of the crisis.* Cambridge, MA: MIT Press.

Drucker, P. (1985). *Innovation and entrepreneurship.* New York, NY: Harper and Row.

Garr, D. (2000). *IBM Redux: Lou Gerstner and the business turnaround of the decade.* New York, NY: Harper Collins.

Gawer, A., & Cusumano, M. (2002). *Platform leadership.* Boston, MA: Harvard Business School Press.

Gibbert, M., Hoegl, M., & Valikangas, L. (2007). In praise of resource constraints. *Sloan Management Review 48*(3), 15–17.

Gilfillan, S. (1935). *Inventing the ship.* Chicago, IL: Follett.

Goller, I., & Bessant, J. (2017). *Creativity for innovation.* London: Routledge.

Granovetter, M. (1973). The strength of weak ties. *American Journal of Sociology, 78,* 1360–1380.

Gundling, E. (2000). *The 3M way to innovation: Balancing people and profit.* New York, NY: Kodansha International.

Harhoff, D., & Lakhani, K. (Eds.). (2016). *Revolutionizing innovation: Users, communities, and open innovation.* Boston, MA: MIT Press.

Henderson, R., & Clark, K. (1990). Architectural innovation: The reconfiguration of existing product technologies and the failure of established firms. *Administrative Science Quarterly, 35,* 9–30.

Imai, M. (1997). *Gemba Kaizen.* New York, NY: McGraw Hill.

Iyer, B., & Davenport, R. (2008). Reverse engineering Google's innovation machine. *Harvard Business Review, 83*(3), 102–111.

Juran, J. (1985). *Juran on leadership for quality.* New York, NY: Free Press.

Lillrank, P., & Kano, N. (1990). *Continuous improvement: Quality control circles in Japanese industry.* Ann Arbor, MI: University of Michigan Press.

Morris, L., Ma, M., & Wu, P. (2014). *Agile innovation: The revolutionary approach to accelerate success, inspire engagement, and ignite creativity.* New York, NY: Wiley.

Osterwalder, A., & Pigneur, Y. (2010). *Business model generation: A handbook for visionaries, game changers, and challengers.* New York, NY: Wiley.

Pinchot, G. (1999). *Intrapreneuring in action — Why you don't have to leave a corporation to become an entrepreneur.* New York, NY: Berrett-Koehler Publishers.

Prahalad, C. K. (2006). *The fortune at the bottom of the pyramid.* New Jersey, NJ: Wharton School Publishing.

Reichwald, R., Huff, A., & Moeslein, K. (2013). *Leading open innovation.* Cambridge, MA: MIT Press.

Rich, B., & Janos, L. (1994). *Skunk works.* London: Warner Books.

Ries, E. (2011). *The lean startup: How today's entrepreneurs use continuous innovation to create radically successful businesses.* New York, NY: Crown.

Rigby, D., Sutherland, J., & Takeuchi, H. (2016a). The secret history of agile innovation. *Harvard Business Review*, (April).

Rigby, D., Sutherland, J., & Takeuchi, H. (2016b). Embracing agile. *Harvard Business Review* (May): 40–46.

Rothwell, R. (1992). Successful industrial innovation: Critical success factors for the 1990s. *R&D Management*, 22(3), 221–239.

Schonberger, R. (1982). *Japanese manufacturing techniques: Nine hidden lessons in simplicity.* New York, NY: Free Press.

Schroeder, A., & Robinson, D. (2004). *Ideas are free: How the idea revolution is liberating people and transforming organizations.* New York, NY: Berrett Koehler.

Schumpeter, J. (2006). *Capitalism, socialism and democracy*. (6th ed.). London: Routledge.

Takeuchi, H., & Nonaka, I. (1986). The new new product development game. *Harvard Business Review*, (January–February), 137–146.

Teece, D., & Pisano, G. (1994). The dynamic capabilities of firms: An introduction. *Industrial and Corporate Change*, 3(3), 537–555.

Teece, D., Pisano, G., & Shuen, A. (1997). Dynamic capabilities and strategic management. *Strategic Management Journal*, 18(7), 509–533.

Tidd, J., & Bessant, J. (2013). *Managing innovation: Integrating technological, market and organizational change*. Chichester: Wiley.

Tidd, J., & Bessant, J. (2014). *Strategic innovation management*. Chichester: Wiley.

Tripsas, M., & Gavetti, G. (2000). Capabilities, cognition and inertia: Evidence from digital imaging. *Strategic management Journal*, 21, 1147–1161.

Tushman, M., & Anderson, P. (1987). Technological discontinuities and organizational environments. *Administrative Science Quarterly*, 31(3), 439–465.

Tushman, M., & O'Reilly, C. (1996a). Ambidextrous organizations: Managing evolutionary and revolutionary change. *California Management Review*, 38(4), 8–30.

Tushman, M., & O'Reilly, C. (1996b). *Winning through innovation*. Boston, MA: Harvard Business School Press.

Utterback, J. (1994). *Mastering the dynamics of innovation*. Boston, MA: Harvard Business School Press.

Von Hippel, E. (2016). *Free innovation.* Cambridge, MA: MIT Press.

Wheelwright, S., & Clark, K. (1992). *Revolutionising product development.* New York, NY: Free Press.

Witte, E. (1973). *Organization für Innovationsentscheidungen.* Gottingen: Schwartz.

Womack, J., & Jones, D. (1996). *Lean thinking.* New York, NY: Simon and Schuster.

Womack, J., & Jones, D. (2005). *Lean solutions.* New York, NY: Free Press.

Zollo, M., & Winter, S. G. (2002). Deliberate learning and the evolution of dynamic capabilities. *Organization Science, 13*(3), 339–351.

INDEX